Wrestling with Adulthood

Wrestling with Adulthood

Unitarian Universalist Men Talk About Growing Up

Edited by Ken Beldon

SKINNER HOUSE BOOKS

BOSTON

Printed in the United States.

Cover design by Robert Delboy
Text design by Suzanne Morgan

ISBN 1-55896-534-3
978-1-55896-534-8

11 10 09 08
5 4 3 2 1

Library of Congress Cataloging-in-Publication Data

Wrestling with adulthood : Unitarian Universalist men talk about growing up / Ken Beldon, editor.
     p. cm.
  ISBN-13: 978-1-55896-534-8 (pbk. : alk. paper)
  ISBN-10: 1-55896-534-3 (pbk. : alk. paper) 1. Unitarian Universalists—Biography. 2. Christian men—Religious life. 3. Christian men—Biography. I. Beldon, Ken.

BX9867.W74 2008
248.8'420882891—dc22
                                        2007038040

Excerpt from "Sometimes a Man Stands Up During Supper," from *Selected Poems of Rainer Maria Rilke: A Translation from the German and Commentary* by Robert Bly, copyright © 1981 by Robert Bly, reprinted with permission from HarperCollins Publishers.

Contents

Foreword

What is young manhood really like? When a man leaves his family of origin and turns his attention to the larger world, what uncertainties and opportunities does he face?

Editor Ken Beldon has brought together a rich, affirming, and gracefully written series of essays by young, religiously liberal men with compelling stories and insights to share. How I wish this book had been available a generation ago, when I first approached adulthood!

What makes this collection so valuable is, most of all, its honesty. These essays are not the inflated boasts of macho men, nor the whining of the defeated. They are, rather, a well-kneaded blend of troubles and triumphs, directly from men who have experienced both.

Beldon acknowledges that the years from eighteen to thirty-five "can be a lonely time." He writes movingly of the breakup of his first marriage, and he aptly compares young adulthood to miles seven through ten in a half marathon: "These are the miles where you run on your own, because the people you began the race with are . . . running their own race, and you can't yet hear the folks at the end cheering you on to the finish."

The essayists tell of their struggles with addictions, love relationships, career changes, and other transitions. James Coomes writes that after he became a dad for the first time, he had to put "one foot in front of the other just to keep my balance." In the end, however, when commenting on the effects of fatherhood, he says flatly: "It is good."

In these pages there are countless nuggets of wisdom for young men, and also value for middle-aged and older readers, especially religious liberals. Explicitly and between the lines, we discover the importance of spirituality to a young adult and how our religious institutions might better serve this important and energetic group.

Older men can also learn of the great significance that young men place on male mentorship. Joseph Santos-Lyons tells the touching story of his relationship with a mentor who guided and nurtured him—and then challenged him to take responsibility for himself and the state of the world. Santos-Lyons considers this relationship one of the great blessings in his life.

Ultimately, it is we, the readers of this book, who are blessed. Indeed, if we are lucky, the young men who think and feel and express themselves in these pages will be among our denomination's, and the world's, next generation of leaders.

Neil Chethik
author, *VoiceMale*

Introduction

According to the old adage, youth is wasted on the young. We associate youth with abundance—an abundance of time, of opportunity, of possibility. We often look back fondly on our younger years, wishing we'd known how good we had it.

But abundance demands more than simple appreciation. As the poet Delmore Schwartz writes, "In dreams begin responsibilities." Great things take root in us in our younger lives, precious longings that can be nurtured. Growing up is a time of taking seriously the claims of our dreams and following them, responsibly, back into life.

The eleven men who contributed their personal stories to this book have crossed the bridge from adolescence into young adulthood. They live in responsible relationship to dreams that express a common vision of mature masculinity, in which men can be mindful, even joyful, stewards of their personal selves.

The choices and variables involved in becoming a man have multiplied. The stories here show the profound impact of feminism on developing professional, familial, and intimate relationships. The writers in this collection refuse to assert damaging ideas of male supremacy or assume guilt for what other men have wrought in thoughtlessness and violence.

Their stories present a third way, a path of deep and sacred connection to the life we all share. In these pages, young adult men wrestle with fidelity, intimacy, integrity, and ethics. Their voices are filled with a soulful hope, a genuine belief that we are called to flourish as human beings and as men. But these stories also remind us that learning to flourish means heeding the lessons of our personal failings—when our dreams proved illusory, or we just weren't ready to claim the full measure of the blessings those dreams could offer.

And so there is one other thing that these eleven men have to tell us—that one of our responsibilities is to keep dreaming anew. Bruce Springsteen sings, "Someday these childish dreams must end, to become a man and grow up to dream again." To truly grow up, each of us has learned how to live in harmony with our dreams, and we still strive to do so.

Ken Beldon

Younger Than That Now

Ken Beldon

My friend's words were exactly what I needed. They were simple and direct and reached way down to soothe me where I felt the worst: "Remember, we're both only thirty-three, and a good deal of the important stuff that's going to happen to us hasn't happened yet." His words were a saving grace, a reminder that what seemed to be a sentence imposed against my life might one day be lifted. Eventually I'd be okay.

This consolation came in response to an e-mail I had just sent to three of my closest friends. I told them of my realization that my marriage, not yet five years old, was coming to an end.

Later that week my wife would move out of the apartment we'd shared, a decision marked by equal parts sorrow, bewilderment, and relief, and for me, by an acute sense of failure. Trained as a minister, I recognized that I was feeling grief for the death of a significant relationship, but this awareness didn't overcome the loss I felt.

The loss was not just that of a person whose presence I would miss, but it was also related to my sense of who I was, or at least who I thought I was going to be. I felt that I had failed to pass one of the essential tests of becoming an adult and a man. It was an odd sensation, though, because instead of feeling young or green with inexperience, I felt old. Not mature or wise, but dirty, spent, ready to be discarded.

For many men, young adulthood (roughly eighteen to thirty-five) is a time of exchanges, of negotiations between various identities. It's a rich occasion for forming and re-forming identity. School is often replaced by work; one's home of origin is replaced by a home of one's creation.

At the same time, men in these years often begin to find greater focus, exchanging the relative freedom of youth for the security and constancy of one particular mate and one particular profession. It is a stage when a young man "buckles down," puts away some of his childhood dreams, and accepts the realities of life.

Sometimes this transition occurs without serious crisis or complaint. But sometimes, the shift between identities is not smooth: The professional identity doesn't materialize, a new geographical location never seems like home, or a significant relationship does not fulfill its promise. In those cases, the deliverance into another identity can seem like emotional exile, a kind of spiritual homelessness in which you can't go back, and yet you're not sure where you're headed.

That was how I felt when my marriage ended. For years I had banked my happiness on the creation of a true home, fatherhood, and a sense of defined place in the world. These seemed to evaporate before me, and as they disappeared, I feared that I might too. I suppose I anticipated that marriage would make me mature. But it takes time to grow into the meaning of the changes we choose for ourselves, and like so many young men, I possessed little patience. And so, when my marriage failed, it felt like a recurring nightmare in which I spilled ink all over a final exam, and it was the only copy I was going to receive.

Although I couldn't hold on to my identity as a husband, the title *Reverend* has stuck with me. My ordination five years before the end of my marriage was not just a very public ritual symbolizing the sacred trust vested in me by a religious people; coming in my late twenties, it was also a rite of passage that separated my youth from my adulthood.

I had always been in a rush to grow up, so I decided to make the time around my ordination a week to remember, and it was. I was ordained on Sunday, learned that I was chosen to be the minister of my first congregation on Thursday, and got engaged on Friday.

I hit the rite of passage trifecta: a title, job, and love. Looking back, I now realize that the staying power of at least two out of three isn't bad.

The title conferred upon me at ordination started me toward where I am today—seven years down the road as a pastor, having served one growth-oriented ministry, and about to begin another. At the celebratory dinner afterwards, my supervising minister and mentor, sensing my mood of happy disorientation, said that even though I now possessed the title *Reverend*, the professional designation would take some time to grow into.

She was right. On that night, and for some time after, I wore the title as I might a new pair of expensive shoes, proudly but not quite comfortably. Only time could make the title become part of my authentic identity.

In his First Letter to the Corinthians, Paul addresses a young religious community in the midst of forming its own spiritual identity. He recognizes their awareness that the gospel has changed their lives, but knows that the full implications of their encounter with religious truth remains unclear. He asks them to have patience and to love one another and he reassures them that eventually all will be made known. After extolling love's virtues, he continues:

> For now we know in part and we prophesy in part, but when the perfect comes, the partial will pass away. When I was a child, I talked as a child,

I thought as a child, I reasoned as a child; *when I became a man, I put away childish things*. Now we see through a mirror, darkly, then we shall see face to face.

(1 Corinthians 13:9–12; italics added)

Paul is addressing a people in transition, a people awkwardly struggling with the responsibilities that attend their new life. As a Unitarian Universalist, I don't share his assurance that every spiritual matter will be laid bare without ambiguity, or that truth will reveal itself unblemished and unquestioned. But I share his hope that self-knowledge and self-identity can be harmoniously reconciled.

Many people in their twenties and early thirties in our culture face a time of letting go, of saying good-bye to well-established ways of relating to the world. They emerge into new patterns of relationship, sometimes with enthusiasm, sometimes with concern. As in so many transitional moments, there is much grief in the farewells of young adulthood. It can be a lonely time. The ties that bind can be pulled in so many directions that they fail to hold tight. Pulled too far or too quickly, they may snap altogether.

As the years of young adulthood pass, friendships can begin to fade. Frequent visits become annual events, no longer nurtured solely by intention and desire, but by the happy accident of a business conference that happens to be geographically convenient.

Once-frequent phone calls become occasional events, and the brief email with a single point of inquiry, typed hurriedly between other commitments, begins to replace the long missive that touches on *everything* that's happening. Hanging out comes to be replaced by just hanging on.

Some relationships ease into being deprioritized; both parties accept that this is just the way of the world. Other relationships rebel against losing their preeminence and becoming consigned to the past. Either way, the emerging identity of adulthood shifts and brings about the tremulous feeling of being on less than stable ground.

As my marriage was ending, I experienced a kind of double loneliness. I was far from where I had grown up, and I felt alienated in the new home that my wife and I had struggled to establish. Perhaps it was this sense of isolation that made me notice the cost of not having a significant relationship—particularly for men as they aged.

At the time, I lived in a South Florida high-rise apartment building whose residents spanned the generations. At one time it had been more exclusively occupied by retired and elderly people. Just about every temperate day, I could look down from my balcony and see gatherings of three or four older women.

They played cards and chatted, presumably of children and grandchildren and medical procedures and the weather and current events and, this being Florida, elections. I saw them going out in small groups for shuttle-bus trips to the mall or heading out to the midday gambling boat. I saw them together.

And then I noticed the aged men, many of them widowers, I imagine. They were often solitary—alone, but someplace where life was. They sat on the bench by the mailboxes, waiting for the afternoon delivery. They lingered in comfortable chairs in the foyer, sometimes with newspapers, sometimes empty-handed. Occasionally they talked with passersby or each other. One regularly offered a Henny Youngman-like pun while riding the elevator, and the younger people smiled uncomfortably at his bygone humor and quickly pressed their floor's button to get where they were going. It was a predictable visual pattern—the older women gathered in groups, the older men on their own.

I wondered how these men had arrived at this place in their lives, after years of doing no doubt very adult things. Time had taken them full circle back to the long lazy hours of childhood, hours that appeared to be so bereft of significant interaction, and I started to grieve for them.

I was also aware that I might have been projecting onto them some of the loneliness I felt at the end of my marriage. Perhaps I was a little panicked that I was staring at some vision of my own future. I committed myself to remember in daily, practical ways the truth of what my friend had told me in his e-mail—that there was a lot of living left to do.

I tried to keep the image of being a child of God before me and came to know a new way of living that phrase, different from the interpretation I had often heard. The phrase did not mean that we should remain in a state of personal immaturity, submissive before God's authority. Rather, it directed me toward a consistent path of awe and wonder, where I didn't see myself or our world by rote, but as something continually created and refreshed through the experience of exploring and receiving reality.

As I started to get over my sense of acute failure, I began to see that I had been living "outside-in" instead of "inside-out," tempted by external symbols of maturity and neglectful of the inner sources of joy that make wanting to be a mature, integrated person a noble goal in the first place. With this realization, I found myself going back in order to go forward. I reached into the depths of my closet and hauled out my old acoustic guitar, restrung it, and started playing—just as badly as when I quit over a decade ago.

My lack of skill didn't seem to matter as much as just having the ability to sit and strum, writing songs about heartache and the end of love, finding the website that had the chord changes to George Jones's "She Thinks I Still Care." Excellence was less important than simple exploration.

Beyond those four walls, I also committed myself to a healthy discipline of running, another youthful joy I had abandoned after an injury. I wasn't a particularly good runner, but that didn't really matter. Running helped me learn the difference between the absence of loneliness and the fullness of solitude. Working my way through ten miles along a quiet beach at night with the stars and the surf around me, I felt a magnificent calm that no anxious longing for companionship had ever brought me.

Even more important, running gave me the ironic and gracious gift of learning to slow down, of focusing on each footfall and deep breath, even the occasional pain and hurt, rather than on the end point. At ten minutes a mile, I wasn't going to be winning any awards anyway, so it was best to take my time and be mindful. Eventually my pace became faster, but that was just the fruit of attentiveness to running, not the goal of the running itself. Running taught me about the abundance of time, rather than its scarcity; that anything done fully in the moment is never started too late. In all my young-adult years of rushing to grow up, I had never felt as if there was enough time. In racing ahead, I had been racing nowhere.

Running also gave me an additional framework of meaning, especially when it came to learning about persistence through difficult times. After running my first half marathon, I encouraged myself during a difficult time several months after my marriage ended: "This is like miles seven to ten. Too far in to feel the rush of novelty, nerves, and adrenaline at the beginning that propelled you forward, too far away to really begin anticipating the end. These are the miles where you run on your own, because the people you began the race with are at their own pace, running their own race, and you can't yet hear the folks at the end cheering you on to the finish. This is the part of the race where your legs really ache, where you doubt if you did the right thing by starting down this path at all. This is the part that is lonely and all you can do is feel the hurt and the strain, focus on your breathing, and dig a little deeper in order to keep moving ahead. It won't always be like this, but this is the way it is now. Accept it and keep going forward."

What running finally did for me was deliver me back to my friends. Several of them are marathoners whose skill level I will never reach, but running has given us a narrative to share, something that binds us across the miles that now separate us. Even more, the gift of slowing down has helped me remember the importance of my friendships and not let them disappear under the weight of other commitments.

Twelve years ago, my five closest friends were romantically involved with different people than those to whom they're now committed. Four are now married, one (me) had been married and is married again, and one had been engaged before the wedding was called off. Two are now parents of toddlers and another is marking his PDA with his wife's ovulation cycles, looking toward conception in the near future.

We were all renters back then. Three of us are now homeowners, and one has already bought the plot of land on which she will retire. Three of us lived together; now none of us lives under the same roof. None of us had the same jobs, or even the same professions, then that we have now.

Nothing symbolizes the stretching of the bonds between us more than the fact that in the autumn of 1994 I lived no more than two hundred miles in any direction from my best friends; we were all along the I-95 corridor between Boston and Washington. A decade later the dots on the map we call home, or have called home, include Fort Lauderdale, Pasadena, Madison, Berkeley, and Belarus.

The period of our early to mid-twenties was one of abundant, easily accessible community, of many hours to sit and talk politics and love and baseball. By the time my marriage ended, I realized how adrift I felt from the community of my friends, simply because so much of the rest of life had intervened. Looking back, those were ten rich years of change that brought much joy to each of us in different ways, but also left a sense of dislocation, one that I particularly felt when my marriage ended. Blessedly, when I reached back for these friendships they were still there, no longer nurtured by frequent contact, but rather by our intention to sustain them.

At one point in my life, when I was painfully earnest about the need to grow up, I would have agreed with Paul's cut-and-dried approach in his letter to the Corinthians: Childish things should be stored away for good, like stuffed animals packed away in a box. Now I see maturation less as a process of exchanging identities and more about incorporating new parts of myself with some of the oldest portions of who I am. I understand that to pack away the things of my youth would have been to ignore a part of my soul.

Unlike the Bar Mitzvah exclamation that I carry from my religious heritage, "Today I am a man!" there is no firm point separating young from old, at least not without achieving an age at too costly a price, and thereby neglecting the wisdom that makes maturity possible.

Certain childish things, like my premature desire to grow up, are best left behind, but having a childlike sense of openness, awe, and deep connection is food for my spirit that I cannot do without. As a child or youth I relished all the times when I was told how mature I was. Yet when my marriage ended, I had one of those "Is that all there is?" moments and decided that I had left too much behind. I needed to dig down gently, like an archaeologist brushing away sediment to free a treasured fossil, to find something lost within me. Fortunately what I found was not just a relic, but the genuine article.

Bob Dylan puts it this way: "Ah, but I was so much older then, I'm younger than that now." For that, I am grateful. No longer do I feel used up and spent. For me the man has been father to the child.

━╾

Ken Beldon serves as lead minister of WellSprings Unitarian Universalist Congregation in Chester Springs, Pennsylvania.

Caught in the Whirlwind

James Coomes

Looking back on when I first started becoming an adult, I realize that my growth process involved completely rearranging my priorities. I gave up some of what I had known and loved in exchange for new things to nurture. Along the way, I had to watch my step. I seemed to be always planting one foot in front of the other just to keep my balance instead of intentionally planning out where I wanted to go.

As a teenager, I was terrified at times, not knowing what I was going to do when I grew up. It seemed to me that my peers all had college plans and intentions to follow in their parents' footsteps; they saw themselves finding a place in the same social worlds they grew up in. As a person of color, I was discouraged from applying to any four-year colleges or universities by my high-school guidance counselor, who warned that I would be setting myself up to fail. I just didn't know what was to become of me. I was anxious to get out from under the shadow of my parents' accomplishments, and I didn't know how.

My father's words gave me hope, and I still cling to them. He said, "Screw what the guidance counselor told you and aim as high as you possibly can—because wherever you end up will be good." This advice has gotten me to where I am today.

But these sage words are a double-edged sword. On the one hand, they required me to assert myself and allowed my ambition to lead me with the faith that everything would turn out alright in the end. On the other hand, they created the risk that I would run too far ahead of myself without thinking things through. My growing up was marked by a startlingly fast series of events, and as they unfolded I wasn't sure I was making all the right decisions.

My entrance into adulthood happened so quickly that I felt out of control. In fewer than ninety days, I bought a home, turned thirty, and became a father. During that same period, the terrorist attacks of September 11 shook me to the core, as they did the entire country. Caught up in a whirlwind of changes, I never took the time to reflect on what it all meant. I could see my old identity quickly disappearing, but felt unprepared for my new roles in a world suddenly changed by previously unimaginable violence.

My wife and I had been living in an apartment complex in South Pasadena, California. Perfectly suited to the lifestyle of a young, newlywed couple, it looked like a re-creation of the Love Boat, with a swimming pool in its center and a lanai providing shade. But when Terri was four months pregnant, we questioned whether it was appropriate for our upcoming responsibilities. Would the baby be able to sleep through the weekend-long parties? Would crying keep our young neighbors up all night during the week? At twenty-nine, we felt surprisingly old in this neighborhood.

We called a real-estate agent to explore whether we could possibly afford to buy a house. What started as a whim quickly took on a sense of inevitability. Within two days of talking with the agent, we met with a mortgage broker, who offered a rate that seemed reasonable at the time. Two days later we found a house we liked, and before we really knew what was happening we entered into an escrow agreement on an 872-square-foot house with a gigantic jungle of a backyard. We had no real idea what we were doing, but it felt like mature, grown-up stuff, and we trusted the people around us.

All I remember of the August evening when my wife and I sat on the front porch holding the keys to our new home was a fear that someone would figure out before nightfall that we were poor. The whole process had taken place so quickly that I was never certain that we did the right thing. At the time, I was also working as a youth coordinator at Neighborhood Church in Pasadena. A recurrent theme of this group was "freedom with responsibility." To some degree, I had incorporated this theme—so while not entirely sure of what we were doing with the purchase of a home, we remained mindful of the process and trusted that since some higher power had granted us with the down payment and appropriate credit score, we were entitled to become homeowners. We were also ultimately responsible for the decisions we made.

We spent the entire month packing and worrying about the escrow and expected to spend September painting, dreaming of furniture we couldn't afford, thinking up baby names, and adjusting to our new status as homeowners. These seemed like the most important issues in our lives.

On the morning of September 11, I was standing in our sparsely furnished living room, waiting for the morning traffic report, when I first heard the news that a terrorist attack was under way. I sat stunned, and then realized that I still had to put one foot in front of the other and go about my day. I had to drive from San Fernando to Los Angeles, where I was to facilitate the start-up of an intensive mental-health service program.

The freeways were eerily quiet. I peered at the sky, questioning whether the drama unfolding three thousand miles away could really be happening. As

I drove past the seventy-three-story Library Tower in downtown Los Angeles, I wondered if it too might be a target. I had never felt so empty and utterly speechless over events I was not directly involved with. Our purchase of a new home, which had dominated my thoughts and emotions for the past few months, suddenly seemed insignificant. I experienced an interconnectedness with others in a way I had never felt before. My personal circumstances seemed insignificant, and my mourning and fear were part of a larger shared consciousness.

That evening, a woman from our neighborhood asked us to light a candle on our porch as part of a vigil. Nothing felt real; the scene seemed scripted for a patriotic movie. Terri and I sat on the steps of our small porch and watched teenagers drive by, draped in American flags. On that night, we were no longer fiscally clueless young adults but patriotic and mournful suburban homeowners, united with our neighbors. Terri and I verbalized a mystery of faith regularly acknowledged by the priests in her home parish. It did not matter in the moment that ours was an interfaith partnership, that we were new to the neighborhood, or that the traumatic events of the day took place three thousand miles away. Our feelings reminded us that we are not removed from the human experiences of others, whether they be in the neighborhood, across the country, or on the other side of the world.

Surprisingly soon, the normal rhythms of life began to take hold again. A few weeks after September 11, I went to play golf with my best friend. I'm not particularly interested in golf, but I enjoyed spending time with him and goofing off. We were splashing balls into a water hazard rather than trying to improve our scores. I found this pursuit particularly entertaining not just because of the actual activity, but because I was now a professional social worker, and the other two in my threesome were a teacher and an accountant. While the mature me would like to say that these activities reflected my need to escape to a younger identity, I believe the truth is that we all have the need to play, regardless of maturity or age.

When we finally tired of the game, we drove to my in-laws' home. As we pulled up, a feeling of disconnectedness came over me. I saw balloons and noticed all the cars parked near the house. Walking up the driveway, I saw people I recognized in the backyard, but I couldn't make sense of what I was seeing—my mom talking to my real estate agent and my boss, a friend from junior high sitting at a table with my sister-in-law and two classmates from graduate school. The static and angst of a Rob Zombie song filled my head as I thought to myself, "This is what it's like when worlds collide."

To celebrate my birthday, my wife had stealthily gathered many people who were very dear to me from different areas of my life. The effect was overwhelming. People who had known me my entire life were mingling with those who knew me only as an adult. On the very day I entered my thirties, I saw my childhood and adulthood merging. All I could do was put one foot in front of the other and join the party.

It was like signing our mortgage papers and processing the traumatic events of two weeks before. I found myself surrounded by a web of support despite feeling as though I was in a free fall. I kept a list of everyone there, sincerely intending to send thank-you cards, but my path has never come to a clearing where I could adequately connect with and thank everyone who made that day possible. Five years later, I'm still waiting to find the right words. The true gift I received that day was learning that my support network is always around me even when it is not tangible.

Eleven days later, I was still recovering emotionally from the party when my wife called to tell me that something was not quite right with the baby. I came home from work to be with her, and we decided to go to the hospital. Once there we were told that Terri and the baby were fine, but some amniotic fluid had begun to leak and the doctor was going to induce labor. The baby wasn't due for two more months. We were in a state of panic and tried to convince the doctor that it just wasn't time yet. We couldn't take in the information we were given about toxemia and the developmental stages of a baby's lungs.

The "induced" labor took place four days later and our daughter Mia was born early on Sunday morning. While we were waiting for the doctor to discharge us, my father-in-law sent me home to take a shower and get the car seat, which was still in its box. With the water running over me, I cried as I had once done in high school when I felt powerless and out of control. But underneath that feeling, I knew there was a higher power flowing through my family and friends, watching over my wife and child and me, keeping us safe. I might be physically alone in any given moment, but time, family, friends, and community would carry me through even if I did not know the next steps I should be taking. I would simply move forward, and all would fall into place.

In the middle of a typical night five years later, I climb out of bed, bleary-eyed and disoriented. My back aches as I try to sit up, and my knees are sore as I put my feet on the floor. I try to navigate, bracing myself for the inevitable slam of my shin against the bed frame. My son is screaming in his crib, his diaper wet. I change him and make my way into the kitchen, while he rests on my shoulder. I prepare a bottle and move to the couch in the living room. As he quietly sucks, I feel his back expand and contract against my chest. I awake a few hours later, feet cold, still lying on the couch, with my head hanging back and my neck twisted to the left. Ethan is on my chest, sleeping blissfully in his flannel pajamas.

Looking out at the first traces of morning, I start to think about the day ahead. Ethan has also woken up, but instead of calling for attention he too is staring out the window. My world revolves around him and his sister, who is blissfully sleeping in their shared room, no doubt dreaming again about a family of elephants named Mommy, Daddy, Mia, and Ethan. Looking at my son's face, I recall similar peaceful moments with my daughter.

In the short ninety-day period during that one year, I used my muscle memory from my own childhood. My parents and family, and uncountable friends and mentors, prepared me for a series of events that I truly believe one cannot prepare for alone. This is a core part of my own spiritual identity. Priorities blur, decision points come too fast to be able to make mindful choices, stress situations lead to stress responses, and true freedom and independence make way for safety, simplicity, and stability. I had no choice but to trust my own father's words from so many years before, advising me to reach out beyond what I could see and trust that I would end up in a good place. Growing up has been about giving up everything I knew and loved, and replacing it with a whole new set of things to know and love. And it is good.

—‑—

James Coomes is a licensed clinical social worker in the field of public mental health in the Los Angeles area and a member of Neighborhood Unitarian Universalist Church in Pasadena, California.

The Larger World

Erik Kesting

My earliest memory is of my father leaving home. My parents divorced before I knew how to tie my shoes. I remember him coming down the stairs and walking out through the front door of our house, a modest brown cape on a dead-end suburban street. With my mother standing beside me at our bay window, I watched him leave in his Chevy pick-up. It was a blue-sky day.

When I started college in Boston sixteen years later it was once again a crisp, clear New England day. My dad helped me move in with his truck and I waved as he left, watching the sun glimmering off the tailgate. It was as if nothing had changed; I was a little boy and he was leaving me behind all over again.

I had less than one week to adjust to my new life away from family before four terrorist attacks exploded my understanding of the world faster than college ever could. When I awoke that morning, only one of the

World Trade Center towers had been hit. Amid the confusion and concern, I felt very keenly how alone I was in this new place. My roommate and I joined others in a neighboring dorm room to watch the events unfold on a small television. We speculated about the perpetrators and the possibility of other planes similarly hijacked and en route to greater disaster. My parents' divorce had taught me early on that my world could be turned upside-down by forces beyond my control, and now that feeling hit me like never before.

My professor stood in front of my introductory biology class; having a more mature understanding of what had happened, he cancelled class. I went outside and tried to reach my family, but cell phone lines were jammed or unavailable so I gathered a few things and drove to my home town of North Andover, Massachusetts, about thirty miles north. My car radio played peace songs from what I had thought was a bygone era. They evoked sharp, unsettling, and visceral feelings. I remember looking at the Boston skyline in my rearview mirror, wondering if it too might soon be fuming black smoke.

I went to my church, its front doors propped wide open with a handwritten sign that read "Sanctuary open to all." A service was scheduled for later that day, but the sanctuary was empty at the time. I sat alone and played hymns at the piano where I had taken some of my first lessons. I had played my first worship service and my first concert there, and its familiarity was soothing. During the service I wept bitterly. Something had changed, in my world and in me.

What I did not realize at the time was that my innocence and idealism passed away that morning. Over time I have been able to grieve and to regain perspective, but I have not recovered the thriving optimism I once championed so strongly. I used to believe that, in my lifetime, the world might find peace and prosperity for all, but now I fear that such hope is naïve. More likely, my generation's greatest contribution will be a small step toward this goal, a small bending of the arc of the universe towards justice.

As the semester rolled on, I found myself reclusive and lost. Returning home for the winter break surfaced my long-suppressed feelings of abandonment and loneliness, growing up as the child of divorced parents. Combined with the uncertainty of beginning college and the shock and tragedy of September 11, these feelings overwhelmed me and I got into a heated argument with my mother and stepfather. In my resentment, I packed a bag and left unannounced.

I spent the next several days with friends and their families, a surreal time filled with home-cooked meals, laughter, and fellowship; young children ran around noisily sharing their excitement for the coming day with anyone who had ears to hear. I played the piano while we all sang carols.

For me, this experience was surreal. It was the family experience I had always wanted. As time passed, I would learn that those picturesque families had their own problems and shortcomings, as all families do. Today, it is painful to think back on those weeks. I must have broken my mother's heart that Christmas.

I yearned for the re-creation of my own family into one of more loving union and understanding, and nothing could replace the emptiness I felt. When things did not improve during the next semester, and after a school year of bitterness and loneliness, I decided it was time to leave.

It was not until I boarded American Airlines flight 146 on July 23, 2002, that I truly entered young adulthood. I was a fresh nineteen years old when my mother drove me to the airport. We prayed together in silence. Then my mother suggested that we pray the Hail Mary three times, a tradition she inherited from her mother and, I think, continued for the comfort of its familiarity. I do not know what else my mother said in her silent prayers, and I do not recall mine, but I am sure they were all earnest words. I remember giving her a hug and a kiss good-bye at the curb. I cannot fathom her thoughts or feelings, but I do wonder if I will someday find myself at that same curb with a child of my own.

I had not purchased a return flight or transportation to my final destination. My soul was taking its first step onto the proverbial open road. I was flying to Paris, then on to Budapest by train. After a two-week conference on religious freedom, I would hitch a bus ride with some American friends across the mountainous border into Transylvania, the northern region of Romania. I would teach English to students from kindergartners to adults, in return for room and board at the parsonage of the First Unitarian Church of Marosvásárhely. In time, I would find much more than room and board—I would find hospitality, friendship, and hope.

I spent four months in Marosvásárhely. When I wasn't teaching my forty young adult and adult students and my twenty kindergartners, I traveled the countryside, visiting with farmers, ministers, doctors, and students and listening to their stories of lives filled with passion and commitment, joy and sorrow.

My hosts, the Nagy family, lived in a modest two-bedroom parsonage in a residential area of the city just a few blocks from the church. Off the back door was a small deck with a slanted plastic roof where they hung clothes to dry in the summer. Grapevines climbed its railings, and in the fall, the grapes were collected in an enormous blue plastic barrel to be fermented into wine. Tall grass surrounded a large garden of tomatoes, eggplant, cucumbers, and other vegetables.

László Nagy was the senior minister; his wife, Gizi, served as the church administrator and coordinator of countless church and community programs and projects. Their children were two of the truest companions for me. Their daughter, Erzsébet, was in high school and her younger brother, Lacika, studied at the city's music school. I always felt comfortable asking them questions about cultural, linguistic, or other things I did not understand. The children shared a bunk bed in their upstairs room, and any new visitors would take my spot on the dining-room futon, while I stayed with Lacika and Erzsébet. Those were memorable nights of storytelling and laughter. With Lacika sleeping on the floor, we couldn't even open the door more than a few inches, but we didn't mind.

The Nagy home was my home too, a place where I learned sincere hospitality. I had a key and was free to come and go, and even to invite guests. Living with their family, I felt truly welcomed and in turn became a far more generous and thoughtful person. Today, this personal growth continues to give me hope, hope that I can change further and that others can too.

A few weeks into my stay, I went to a conference in a nearby village while the Nagy family took a trip to Hungary. I would be home several days before them, which would not have been a problem except that I returned violently ill. On the last night of the conference, I had accidentally eaten undercooked meat. I took only a few bites before realizing, but it was too late. Keeping the contents of my stomach where they were while on the dirt roads back from the village was a challenge I did not soon forget. Getting back to the parsonage provided some relief to my anxiety—if not to my stomach. I called my mother, and though she sympathized, there was little she could do for me from the other side of the globe.

I thought about going to the hospital and decided against it. The sharp disparity between medical care in the United States and Romania, and many other poorer nations, is impossible to appreciate without firsthand observation. This was something I had seen on many trips to the hospital as a visitor, not a patient. Having only eaten a little of the undercooked food I was better off than some of my friends at the conference, and I slowly rehydrated myself. I learned from this experience that just because something terrified me did not mean it was going to kill me. I realized that although it would have been nice, no one really needed to be there with me. I endured on my own. And I found out that the independence I sought was horrifically scary for a teenager.

I took teaching very seriously, thoroughly preparing my lessons while leaving room for appropriate spontaneity. At the beginning of each class, I had the students write journal entries about whatever was going on in their lives, a technique I had learned in high school from my favorite language teacher. Their journals showed me how they were progressing, and my feedback on grammar and spelling helped them learn everyday English. I felt the power of authority as a teacher and, with it, an enormous responsibility to do the very best for my students. My commitment to excellence earned me their respect, and their hard work earned them mine. Discovering something important that I could do well, I gained great confidence, for which I am grateful.

After I had settled in for a few weeks, Gizi decided that the family would speak to me only in Hungarian. Her intent was to help me to learn Hungarian, but I think it was also a challenge for me to realize how hard my students were working to learn my language. I quickly appreciated her decision, as my increased fluency helped me learn more about Hungarian culture and made daily living easier. Transylvanian Hungarians already have to learn Romanian since it is the state language. They usually study one or two additional languages, as early as middle school. I began to understand the privilege of speaking not only the dominant language in my country, but also a globally spoken language. I began to understand a lot about privileges during my time there.

The family and the friends I made in Transylvania built my confidence. They believed in me. They helped me organize travel plans and introduced me to many great people. They even arranged for me to give a special piano concert in the city's citadel! The generosity of the Nagy family and others who hosted me during my stay was unrivaled by any I had experienced before. I learned that true happiness is not defined by wealth or success. It is defined by love and quality of character. It is defined by family and friendship. What was most powerful, affecting, and memorable about my experience with the Nagy family, and my other hosts, was their incomparable hospitality and generosity. They gave up their own beds for me, prepared meals for me day after day, listened to me, and taught me with patience and kindness. I learned how it feels to receive deep hospitality and how to be deeply generous.

Young adulthood thus far has deeply challenged my personal identity, my creativity, and spirituality; it has encouraged me to work harder to bring beloved community into the world. My trip to Eastern Europe made me aware of the suffering of the larger world; it also taught me that love endures even in the world's darkest corners.

I connected with the people in Transylvania in a way that changed my mental categorization of them as "other" and thus restored my hope for and commitment to the prospect of peace. I learned gratitude. I learned that I am fortunate. I learned the benefits of a generous heart, hard work, and faith. I learned to complain less.

When I returned to the States, I was eager to reunite with my family. It would take time and patience to build the relationships I yearned for, but I had experienced a powerful change of self. Instead of just being angry at the past, I would create new opportunities. I realized that the responsibility for my familial relationships belonged to me more than to anyone else.

I will be twenty-four when this text goes to print. Since my trip, I have worked to become more honest, patient, and loving with all the people I encounter. I hope that my personality is accented by boldness and generosity. Today, I realize the enormous value of my opportunity to travel to Transylvania. My awareness of this privilege informs my understanding of the world, deepens my gratitude, and calls me to action. Most important, whenever I think of my experiences in Transylvania, I am reminded that success and happiness are defined not by income or renown, but by love and quality of character, by family and friendship.

— —

Erik Kesting is the young adult and campus ministry assistant at the Unitarian Universalist Association of Congregations and a student at Harvard Divinity School.

Being the Change I Want to See

Joseph Santos-Lyons

My fear of change is like my fear of needles. I spend more time worrying about it than the process actually takes. But change is inescapable, a constant reality that we all struggle to understand and endure. Facing it, I assess my strengths and weaknesses, analyze the positives and negatives, and speculate about my future, all while trying to carry on with my normal routine.

Mahatma Gandhi said, "You must be the change you want to see in the world." These words speak to me because in my life personal and social change have always been linked. As I have grown personally, I have awakened to societal oppressions that affect us all. And as I have worked on issues of social justice, I have found opportunities to grow into an adult man.

Change is one of the paradoxes of life, and I greet it with both fear and hope. I continually graduate into new beliefs, relationships, and identities, but still fight to keep what I know. I have difficulty adopting new ways of being in a world that is saturated with materialism and oppression. I recognize that struggle within myself and strive to prepare myself for constant and inevitable change, to remember and feel my connections with the past, present, and future of life and creation. This internal grounding readies me for the experience of loss that accompanies change and reminds me that the change I seek is good, just, and moral, even as I remain a work in progress.

Growing up, I lived an economically privileged life. My father was the primary wage earner, and my mother was able to spend significant time at home with my sister and me. My family and community supported and encouraged each step of my development, and they had the material means to do so.

I entered college full of confidence and passion for life. The surge of independence that came with moving away from home, even just forty-five miles, was powerful. I made new friends, and we bonded over coffee and late-night discussions. In the midst of the excitement, I felt as though I was on a roller coaster, afraid of what would come next but not wanting to get off.

Looking back now, I realize that I was going through major spiritual and psychological changes at the time, but I focused on all of the external changes to avoid the complexity of what was changing inside me. With the energy of youth, I even pursued my spiritual journey as a kind of superficial quest. I poured myself and my anxiety into an unrestrained search for truth and meaning that didn't touch the real me.

Unitarian Universalism was a critical part of my life at this point. I became involved in continental Young Religious Unitarian Universalists (YRUU) and served on the YRUU Steering Committee. With these experiences, I learned as much about my attitudes and behavior toward others as I did about youth leadership.

College was nothing like I expected. I knew that it was expensive and that I should take full advantage of it, but I had trouble settling on a major. My original path as a music major ended after my first semester at Willamette University, and I then spent a quarter at a community college before transferring to the University of Oregon in Eugene. During my time at Willamette, I became engrossed with the Clarence Thomas confirmation hearings, which became a key event in my personal development.

In the fall of 1991, Anita Hill, a law professor at the University of Oklahoma, accused Clarence Thomas, nominee for the U.S. Supreme Court, of sexual harassment. I was gripped by the story, which raised the interlocking issues of race and gender, and I followed it closely.

At first, I was undecided about Hill's accusations. Yet as I continued to watch the testimony I came to question my previously unexamined belief that it's best to be blind to identity and power relationships. I woke up to the reality of oppression. Nearly all my fellow students were either indifferent or antagonistic to Hill's claims, and I felt intense peer pressure to side against her. I remember sitting alone watching the hearings while other students jeered at me or urged me to turn the channel to sports. I knew then that I wanted to be part of a community that shared a deep sense of justice and collective action. I decided to leave Willamette. Once I was gone, I spoke often of the injustice of the confirmation hearings with my parents, friends, and members of my church. I drifted further from both my high school friends and music communities because of the ways they reacted. Although I no longer talk much about the impact of Anita Hill's testimony on me, it is an important part of who I am today.

Another experience that challenged and changed me happened during my time at the University of Oregon. In many ways it was my first authentic understanding of what it means to be a man in this society.

With my women friends, I thought I had come a long way toward being genuine and caring. Nevertheless, whatever issue was at stake, I was likely to think, "We don't have time to spend on the intricacies of gender politics. We're focused on our goals and they are the most important thing." I felt immune to criticism, and somewhat self-righteous.

A number of my friends were women of color who were heavily involved in racial justice efforts. Through them, I learned of my own patterns of chauvinism, habits of superiority that manifested in my communication and physical presence. Two in particular took time to talk with me on a Friday, giving me the weekend to reflect. They spoke of my patting women on the shoulders or head, creating a feeling of paternalism, and of the way I judged women's comments compared to those of men in our workplace, the Multicultural Center.

It wasn't an easy conversation, but I worked hard to listen and remember. I came to realize that I had understood the issue only superficially. My view of gender as a question of individual human equality had not done enough to educate me to the powerful forces of gender bias that permeate our customs and norms.

Although I got defensive at times, with the support of close friends who took the time to speak about their concerns and frustrations, I found the courage and vision to redefine myself. While no perception is perfect, their feedback gave me a window into my attitudes and behavior and helped me move myself into a more appropriate, gentle, and authentic place.

Another life-changing event also took place during my college years. I ran into a long-time youth advisor and adult mentor who had served with me on the youth/adult committee. Having an adult male mentor in my life had been a blessing—a relationship that challenged me and gave me a positive role model. I had developed my connection with him slowly outside of our committee meetings, generally under the pretense of talking about Unitarian Universalist business. We'd talk on the phone now and then, primarily about the politics and activities of the youth community. He was always a great advisor and provided critical and sometimes bluntly honest feedback. He wasn't always popular because he had a somewhat surly attitude. I really pushed for our relationship and made lots of efforts to contact him, and he was always great about responding. He was honest with me and discussed at length with me the importance of boundaries, ethics, and right relationship. He was someone I envisioned staying in touch with for my whole life, though I imagined our relationship would keep changing as I changed and grew.

We met for lunch and after exchanging pleasantries and briefly catching up, he crisply informed me that our relationship as I knew it was over. I was stunned. My first reaction was to feel that I had done something wrong and that he was upset. He told me that I was not a youth anymore and that he was not my youth advisor. He said we could still stay connected, but that things would be very different. After my initial shock, I realized his words felt right. Although I felt the loss that accompanied this change, I sensed it was a kind of coming of age. I was losing part of our strong bond and knew that a new effort and new framework for our friendship would be needed.

I wasn't sure what to say. He called my attention to the change in my life, to the bridge I was crossing, before I was even aware of it. He helped me see that I was growing up. I now seek to have this kind of impact on others. I try to create the space for similar encounters in my work with young adults.

Once I had recovered from my lunch companion's announcement, we talked about my future, what my interests were, and where I might go. After a lot of listening and questions, he offered a simple piece of advice. I had been talking a lot about community organizing; I was interested in political science and working with groups of people. With his usual quirky bluntness, my mentor told me to find opportunities to learn about money. "Follow the money," he said, "and you will understand power."

This was my introduction to the privileges of power, a concept I had learned quickly on an economic level since my parents had declared bankruptcy, and soon came to understand more universally through the communities I became part of. My mentor encouraged me to understand power through the thread of managing finances. I followed this line of thinking, tentatively, and found a richness both in the clarity of his comments and in the reality of my experience. This grounded me as I more intentionally became a leader and activist within Unitarian Universalism and the community.

My experiences with race and gender are linked to multiple other learnings, including the intersections of oppressions and the power of cultural norms. We cannot escape this by viewing individuals as unconnected to those who share a similar identity. To understand and love one another, we must know that identity oppression and cultural marginalization deny the need for a collective response to a collective problem.

My journey as a progressive man will last a lifetime. I strive for accountability with all the people in my life, in my work, and in my community. Then I have my own work to do—to become in spirit an opponent of all forms of domination and oppression.

My fear of change, like my fear of needles, has lessened over time. Through my interest in social justice, I am not the man I once was, nor the man I will become. In order to be the change I want to see in the world, I continue to examine both my own spiritual life and the systems of power in the culture around me. The changes in me and the changes I can make in the world are part of the same process of maturity. May they continue to be so.

——

Joseph Santos-Lyons is a Unitarian Universalist minister and currently serves as executive director of the Northeast Coalition of Neighborhoods in Portland, Oregon.

Wrestling Matches

Anthony David

As I consider my struggles to grow into greater maturity, I think of wrestling with the men in my life, especially my father. Despite all the difficulties of this process, if I had stepped back from these struggles, I think that a part of me would have died.

Men have been living this story ever since the beginning. It's the ancient tale of Jacob wrestling with the angel. Jacob's life is in danger. The risks he has taken, the things he has done to make his way in the world, are coming back to haunt him. One night when Jacob is alone, a figure appears out of nowhere, and the two wrestle throughout the night. As the light dawns, Jacob realizes that the being he had been wrestling is no man but an angel from God. The angel says, "Let me go, for the day is breaking," and Jacob replies, "I will not let you go, unless you bless me." In this way, Jacob is initiated into his destiny in life, and the angel gives him a new name to signify the momentous transition. The new name is Israel.

"I will not let you go, until you bless me." We wrestle with the male figures in our lives: our fathers, our mentors, the people who have both helped and harmed us. Through this process we are initiated into the mystery of our own authority and authenticity. This is how we find the golden thread of our destiny. A man must wrestle the angel and be given a new name. He must, or part of him dies.

How many times have you heard it said, "I don't want to make the same mistakes that my parents made. I want to do better with my son or daughter than my own parents did with me"? I've said it myself many times. Even now I cannot renounce these words. Fathers and mothers, even the best of them, with the best of intentions, hurt us and scar us. At times the inner parent pops out and says, "You just wait! Just wait 'til you have your own children, and then you'll see what it's like!"

As bad as those wounds might be, our fathers and father figures are part of a past that has formed us, and we must not turn our backs upon that past. There have been times when I tried hard to make my memories disappear, but the end result was not liberation, not more freedom. It was, rather, a feeling of living in limbo, of existing nowhere, of being a mere abstraction. It is fatherhood, ultimately, that has taught me to affirm my father and to love him, even as I struggle with his memory and my need to wrestle a blessing out of him.

My dad was a workaholic, the kind of guy who always said, "If you're gonna do it, do it right or not at all." I remember him as truly alive only when he was at work, wearing his crisp white lab coat with his name stitched on it: Dr. Robert Makar. People loved him. He never talked down to anyone, never rushed through an exam. He always gave his total loving attention to patients, answered all their questions, knew their names. But when he came home, he was dead tired, falling asleep at the dinner table. Not really there.

When I was younger, Dad would tell my brothers and me about his adventures as a mad-scientist kid who experimented with chemicals and burned a hole in his sister's bed or blew up this or that. There were stories about his days as a Boy Scout and eventually as Queen Scout, the Canadian equivalent of an Eagle Scout. Dad knew how to have Dennis-the-Menace fun with chemicals and how to tie a knot fifty different ways, but he never showed us these things. He was too busy working.

When I think of my father, a story comes to mind. A mother and her nine-year-old son were at a grand concert hall, tuxedos and evening dresses everywhere, a high-society extravaganza. Paderewski, the famous composer and pianist, was scheduled to perform, and the mom had hopes that her son would be encouraged to play the piano if he could just hear the immortal master at the keyboard.

The boy was fidgety, and as the mom turned to talk to her friends, he slipped away from her side, irresistibly drawn to the concert grand Steinway on the huge stage. Seemingly unnoticed, he sat down at the tufted leather stool, staring wide-eyed at the black and white keys. He placed his small, trembling fingers in the right location and began to play "Chopsticks." The conversational buzz hushed as hundreds of frowning faces turned in his direction. The crowd began to shout: "Get that boy away from there!" "Who'd bring a kid that young in here?" "Where's his mother?" "Somebody stop him!"

What a moment of reckless hope! The boy could stay seated in the audience no longer; he had gotten up and walked right out there onto the stage for all to see. But in those moments before he got up, he must have felt the overwhelming pressure of the expectation that he would sit quietly and listen like everyone else.

I too know what it's like to feel that I'm supposed to stay in my seat, stuck fast, defeated before I even make a move. For many of us, it is a legacy from our families, a legacy that can make it so hard to walk onto the stage and play whatever piece of music is ours to play.

In my high-school yearbook, someone wrote, "To our president with the funky lookin' glasses. I wish you the best of luck in everything you do. I know you will come out on top." But what happened instead was the real world. I went to college, and then to graduate school. Got a job teaching philosophy. And strangely enough, my own workaholism crept up on me. Every lecture had to be excellent, a model of wisdom, and because philosophy is difficult for many students, I worked extra hard to make it interesting—and possibly even fun.

And while I was hard at work, I was fighting off feelings of being a big fake. Here I was, a philosophy professor, but did I fully understand Socrates, Plato, Aristotle, and Nietzsche? "If I'm gonna do this," I said to myself, "I'd better do it right or not at all." The voice of my father, always in the back of my mind.

It's not that I didn't love what I did, but it was hard to go out there and play "Chopsticks" poorly. So I worked. And worked. And worked.

You can imagine what I was like when I came home.

It was as if what I saw my dad do every day was already deep inside me. It felt natural, what I knew best. Dad working like a dog. Dad coming home tired. Dad falling asleep at the drop of a hat. Dad up early the next day, off to work.

The poet William Blake writes that in life, "joy and woe are woven fine." To me, this line describes the human condition. Not black and white, but shades

of gray, joy and woe woven together so finely that if
you tried to remove all the woe, the joy would go as
well. So too are love and hurt and healing woven. The
people who love us most can hurt us most; yet it is out
of these same hurts that we can find strength to heal
other people and ourselves.

I continue to discover this truth through fatherhood—my own starting in 1992, but also how it reso-
nates with my dad's fathering of me, how my voice is
still connected to his even though he has been dead for
years. His fathering of me goes on, a gathering of love
and hurt and healing woven fine.

Sometimes when I talk to my daughter, I hear his
perfectionism in my voice. One morning several years
ago, I was walking nine-year-old Sophia to school, and
we were late. Feeling anxious, I told her to hurry up.
Halfway there, I noticed that the laces of her sneakers
were untied, flopping all over the place and turning
brown in the muddy slush of Chicago's springtime.
Now, in addition to being anxious, I was irritated. And
then worried. I thought, "If I don't say something about
this, she's gonna grow up taking things for granted!"

Anxiety, irritation, worry: a potent mix of emotions.
Way too harshly, I told her, "Sophia, you need to tie
your shoelaces." She stopped walking, turned slowly
to face me, stared me down in a way that I am told *I*
sometimes stare people down, and said "No!" She was
fed up with all my poking and prodding.

But I was fed up, too, and scolded her. "You might trip yourself up and you need to take care of what you have!" I knew my voice was louder than necessary but I couldn't seem to control it.

Sophia stalked off, furious. I stood there, watching her small form recede into the distance toward her school. As my irritation subsided, a terrible sheepish feeling came over me.

The angel on my right shoulder whispered, "Why are you being so controlling?" but the devil on my left was stiff with self-righteousness. Couldn't let it alone, couldn't walk away. And I gave in. I heard myself calling after her, "You just wait 'til you have your own children, and then you'll see what it's like!" These were the last words Sophia heard as she slipped through the front door of Ray Elementary School.

There I was, channeling my father, passing on all the hurts I had experienced in my upbringing. When I realized this, standing there on a Chicago street in the midst of a messy spring day, I felt overwhelmed with a sense of betrayal. People who were supposed to love me the best hurt me the most, and here I was, inadvertently passing on the hurt.

And then I became afraid. Dad hadn't been perfect for me, so how was I going to be perfect for my kid? And yet, there is that vision—joy and woe woven together. So finely that you can't separate them.

We just can't forget the joy. When I was at seminary

at the University of Chicago, every Wednesday one of the food courts would sell milk shakes at the bargain price of one dollar. Sophia and I were regulars; it was bonding time for us. It reminded me of when my dad and I would hang out. Usually Sophia and I ate dinner first, and when she put her order in, I'd watch as she stood on tiptoe to speak above the counter. I'd listen to her songbird voice and remember a time when she was more likely to wear her food than eat it.

We'd eat and chat, and I'd ask, "What's going on? How's life?" She'd tell me about her friends and share the latest jokes.

Knock knock.
Who's there?
Canoe.
Canoe who?
Canoe help me with my homework?

She'd talk about fifth grade, and I'd talk about seminary. She'd gripe about one of her yucky teachers, and I'd gripe about one of my yucky professors.

Joy and woe. They just go together. And now it is back to a woe. Once, Sophia and I were arguing, and I asked her to help me understand where she was coming from. She snapped back, "Dad, you will *never* understand me!" When things cooled down, she told me that she didn't mean it, that it had to do with the fact that I wasn't a girl, so I wouldn't be able to understand like Mom. And how could I disagree? But it did not take away my loneliness for her. It did not take away my memory of standing there helpless, in silence, not knowing what to say.

Silence settles around the issue of work as well. As a minister, I identify with the poet Rilke when he says,

> Sometimes a man stands up during supper
> And walks outdoors and keeps on walking,
> Because of a church that stands somewhere in
>   the East.

A vision of Truth, of God, of Life Abundant grasps me, and I go where I am sent. Yet I am anguished about the time it takes away from being with family. I think of my resentment of my father's work and wonder how Sophia can understand. Medical school taught my father to be a fine doctor, and the world honored him for that, but it did not teach him how to be a father. The world made it difficult for him to juggle the two responsibilities.

Sophia was nine when my dad died at the age of sixty. He had a sudden heart attack in the middle of the night. I tried to talk to her about death, what it means to live in the face of one's inescapable end. Before we got very far, though, Sophia chided me: "Dad, you're getting too serious again!" And that's okay. There's only so much philosophizing and theologizing you can do with a nine-year-old, although I yearned to share my thoughts with Sophia. I still do, and I always will.

My father's death catapulted me into a place I could never have imagined, and I'm still feeling it. It's the kind of grief people never really get over, though over time we learn to live with it differently.

And it takes us continually to unexpected places. It takes us right back home. That's where it's taken me. It's grounded me in my past and in myself. Son of a father, father of a daughter.

The wrestling match is worth it. Looking back on my relationship with my father, I feel perhaps what that kid felt on the stage, with everyone yelling at him.

It's time to hear the rest of the story now. The boy and his mom were at the concert hall to hear the great Paderewski perform. Backstage, the master overheard the sounds out front and quickly put together in his mind what was happening. Hurriedly, he grabbed his coat and rushed onstage. Without a word, he stooped over behind the boy, reached around both sides, and began to improvise a countermelody. As they played together, Paderewski kept whispering in the boy's ear: "Don't quit. Keep on playing . . . don't stop."

And so it is with every person alive. We are all trying to do better than our parents, trying to come out on top. But when we get out there onto the stage and start playing, what comes out isn't the fantasy in our heads. We find ourselves playing the same old tunes our parents played. It's not totally new and fresh. It's . . . "Chopsticks," and not very well played, either. We hear the catcalls from the audience. And we discover that we are our own worst enemies, saying to ourselves: *You didn't come out on top. You didn't.*

But listen for these words, too: *Don't quit. Keep on playing . . . don't stop.* Whoever we are, we deserve to hear them. God says them to me. Not literally, as if we're talking on the phone. But I feel the Spirit of Life in myself, in nature, in the universe, and it's deeper than ego, it is Hope, it is Love. It tells me that my identity and my journey through life are larger than I can comprehend. It says, *You are here to do something. Don't judge yourself. Play your "Chopsticks." Start there, and then work through it and move on. Forgive yourself.*

These are precious words that all people need to hear—especially in the face of regrets and the perplexities of existence. We play the tune we are born to, or given, or create, but something stands with us, improvising a countermelody, whispering in our ears to keep going, that we are exactly where we need to be at the moment. Perhaps the words come from a spouse or partner, a friend, a group of supporters, a community, or God.

Don't quit. Keep on playing . . . don't stop. That's what moves us into maturity. Voices of encouragement and hope, voices of renewal, so that a generation later

we can return to the sweet shining hopes of our youth
and still believe, still say, "I wish you the best of luck in
everything you do. I know you will come out on top."

━ ━

Anthony David is senior minister of the Unitarian
Universalist Congregation of Atlanta, Georgia.

Receiving Grace

Kent Matthies

Life was a struggle for me in my early twenties. I was constantly sad. When I cried I felt better because I released some of the pain, but that wasn't enough, and I drank too much. Now I know that the depression that runs in my family was affecting me as well. But during my senior college year I couldn't explain the sadness that came over me. My high-school and early college years had been filled with fun, friends, and growth, yet suddenly I felt like I had been handcuffed and thrown into Lake Michigan. It took everything I had to keep my head above water, and I was utterly exhausted. Due to some combination of natural and social causes, I felt a deep void in my life.

Growing up, I had a loving, supportive family. We ate dinner together every night, gathered around the kitchen table, discussing politics. We had good family friends and we went on vacations. We attended Third

Unitarian Church of Chicago and enjoyed the superb preaching of Rev. Donald Wheat, who taught that celebration, gratitude, and generosity were keys to living a good life.

In my late teens, I began to feel disconnected from the church, even though I still believed what I learned there about how to be a good person. As it does for so many young UUs, church became boring and uncool. I immersed myself in other activities, some healthy and others not. I went to a small liberal arts school, Lawrence University, in Appleton, Wisconsin. There I turned away from sports, which had been a preoccupation in high school, in favor of the excitement of social causes. The Reagan administration's human rights abuses and preferences for the rich outraged and energized my peers and me, and we devoted ourselves to change. We became involved in the Sanctuary Movement, working to bring illegal refugees from Central America to our campus for protection and to speak out about the oppression in their homeland. In protest against apartheid, we tried to persuade the board of our school to divest from companies doing business in South Africa.

One of the highlights of my college experience was when several of us built a plywood shanty in the center of the campus quadrangle. During the ice-cold Wisconsin winter, we took two-week shifts living in the shanty. Trying our best to demonstrate solidarity with poor, disenfranchised folks in South Africa, we slept outside with no electricity or heat—but we had lots of sleeping bags and great conversations about how much we wanted to improve the world.

In the fall semester of my senior year, I studied in Costa Rica, where I met hundreds of Nicaraguans at a United Nations refugee camp. To my amazement, most of them had fought on the side of the U.S.-backed contras, whom I vehemently opposed. Meeting people with whom I disagreed politically opened my mind. I had assumed that contras were mean, cold, and senseless, but these people were kind, loving, and generous. They welcomed me into their homes and shared their meals, photos, and stories with me. The world was not as black and white as I had supposed.

Costa Rica also provided lots of partying. Beer, tequila, and *guaro* (hard liquor) were plentiful, and my drinking, heavy for years, became excessive. I was fluent in Spanish, but I remember getting into a taxi late one night in San Jose and finding myself unable to speak to the driver. The next day I took a cold shower, and as the water hit my body, I realized that I had been in an alcoholic stupor and could have died. I couldn't even tell how close I had come. I also wasn't sure that I wouldn't drink the same amount, or more, again.

My parents came to visit me in Costa Rica over the holidays. My mother and I fed bananas to monkeys. We saw huge rocks covered with large, colorful iguanas baking in the sun, and we snorkeled in the coral reefs among fish glowing red, blue, and yellow. But in the midst of this natural beauty, with people I loved dearly, I felt tremendously alone. It was like being encased in a thick plastic bubble that prevented me from experiencing the love and support my family offered. In hindsight, I think of this time as my alcoholic bottom.

When I returned to the States, I began to see a counselor regularly, trying to identify the issues or experiences in my life that were keeping me from finding peace and happiness. The counselor put me on an antidepressant drug, but I was drinking so much that I wasn't getting any better. At a program called Alcohol Behavior Consulting, I joined a group of twenty-five people, most of whom had been ordered to participate by a judge. In the middle of the five-week program, we agreed to spend two weeks without drinking or drugs. The best way to describe this experience is "white knuckling"—I often had to exert all my emotional and spiritual strength not to drink. Although I was proud that I kept my end of the bargain with the group, I was also thrilled when I could go back to drinking at the end of the two weeks. I knew in my heart that someday I would have to seriously revisit my drinking, but I decided that it wasn't realistic to think I could finish my senior year without it. My habits of going to bars with certain people felt too entrenched for me to stop. I committed to drinking beer for the most part and limited the tequila and vodka, because hard liquor often made me feel like I was smashing into a brick wall.

One of the ways I tried to get back to center was by attending the Unitarian Universalist Church of Appleton, Wisconsin. Rev. Roger Bertchausen was a kind, warm pastor who gave me support. I learned of a UU student group at Lawrence, and willing to try anything, I attended. One weekend, on a retreat in the woods, we sat on a hill watching stars and I saw the planet Mars for the first time. I was so amazed to see something so unbelievable that I felt hopeful; maybe I could find peace and joy again.

After college I moved to Washington, D.C., where I met people who showed me the way to recovery. Getting to know who I really was often felt like going into a dark and cluttered attic without a flashlight. It was overwhelming and often seemed hopeless, like there was no way I could ever clean up the mess of fear, low self-esteem, and pain I was in.

But I found new friends in the process, and I learned how to tell my truth and how to ask for help. People loved me and showed confidence in me, even when I came up short. I learned how to pray and followed a program of self-reflection, commitment to positive change, asking forgiveness, and letting go of things I can't control. I also learned that alcohol could never fill the void in my soul. My new community of friends had learned these same lessons and shared the same values. And a couple of my friends from childhood were with me too, without pause.

I began to form unconditional relationships of love and care with men, which allowed me to chip away at the shame I felt around my loneliness. I had come to believe that sobriety was boring, but one of my buddies in early sobriety was committed to disproving this idea, and his attitude was contagious. Since I have been sober, I have enjoyed spending time with friends, making delicious meals, dancing, attending great concerts, and streaking on a frozen Wisconsin lake on New Year's Eve.

Developing male friendships also helped me become more comfortable in my romantic relationships with women. My search for the ideal had never been fair to the women I dated, and I never found what I was looking for. Learning to talk about my real feelings with other men removed the pressure of finding the perfect woman to make my life complete. I was able to feel okay about myself without needing the approval of a woman.

This period of healing was also the beginning of my involvement with spiritual discipline and relaxation. Over the years, this commitment has grown into a regular practice of prayer, yoga, talking to friends, reading, and taking bubble baths. I still don't take as much time for myself as I would like, but when I do I treasure it.

At that time I had a good friend who had been writing to me about her transformative experiences working with refugees in Latin America. At the age of twenty-four, I moved to Chiapas, Mexico, as part of her organization, Witness for Peace. We worked with people from the United States, Mexico, Guatemala, and beyond. Meeting others who made sacrifices to be with refugees in a foreign land inspired me. We worked with Catholic bishop Samuel Ruiz, one of the greatest liberation theologians in Latin America, who had for decades put his life at risk by challenging business and military powers in southern Mexico. He was a humble, kind, and gentle soul who continually returned to the danger zones. I will always treasure the two occasions on which I got to meet him and give him a hug.

I remember one occasion when a delegation of twenty people from the United States visited a camp where I had strong friendships with the refugees who lived there. Like hundreds of thousands of Guatemalans, most of these refugees had fled intense political violence, including massacres, kidnappings, and torture. Many had left their homes with whatever they could carry in their hands and on their backs. Over many weeks they had walked through cold mountains and slept in the brush. At the camp where they now lived, the refugees brought their marimba instruments out of storage for the first time in years in order to throw a party for the visitors. On the day of the event, thick sheets of rain poured across the compound, but the hosts quickly constructed a pavilion with tarps and sticks. We danced together in mud so thick it covered our ankles. Most of the delegates spoke no Spanish and the refugees spoke no English, yet smiles, laughter, and dance were clear languages of joy.

Standing with the poor has taught me profound lessons about gratitude, generosity, and courage. In the refugee camps I clearly heard my call to ministry. At twenty-six, I came home to Chicago to recover from typhoid. I also entered seminary and have never questioned the call since then. Four years later, I was ordained. Ministry has brought me to jails and connected me with young gang members not yet in jail, trying to avoid violence, imprisonment, and death. It has allowed me to work with college students and young adults on their journeys of faith and has brought me to the parish, where we cradle babies, help the elderly die, and do every blessed thing in between.

Looking back, I see a pattern of relationships with clergy members who befriended and guided me through my twenties and early thirties, and my home church was another important factor in my call to ministry. On the sanctuary walls of Third Unitarian of Chicago are likenesses of Mahatma Gandhi, Martin Luther King, Harriet Tubman, Jesus, Buddha, Susan B. Anthony, and many others—role models who provided the same religious grounding at our church that the immaculate conception and resurrection provide in Christian churches. This early encouragement to social action and public witness has continually helped me decide how to spend my time and energy in meaningful ways.

We called the Sunday morning service at our church "Celebration of Life." As I grew into young adulthood, I came to understand and embrace the importance and power of this message. In my last year before seminary, still working with refugees, I had grown increasingly angry at the world and especially the people and government of the United States. I then came to realize that anger is not a sustainable fuel for life. Unitarian Universalism teaches that the resilience of the human spirit is amazing. Even when we dedicate our lives to being aware of pain and injustice, we can find wellsprings of renewal—eating dinner by candlelight, having a picnic in the woods, listening to a Mozart concerto, or playing a game of basketball.

I am now thirty-eight years old and in my ninth year of full-time professional Unitarian Universalist ministry. It is my honor to serve the Unitarian Society of Germantown, Pennsylvania, a growing, caring, increasingly vibrant community of dedicated and talented folks. Together we have experienced joys and tragedies, and last year we celebrated our 140th anniversary as a congregation. Many of us are highly dedicated to the future of Unitarian Universalism.

This religion, which is based in love, courage, and hope, helped me to save myself. I recently married a woman of grace, soul, and beauty. My journey to this point has made me spiritually strong enough to be in this relationship, and we hope that starting our own family will be a grace-filled experience that reflects our gratitude for all the miracles of existence.

Life is full of glory!

━━

Kent Matthies is minister of the Unitarian Society of Germantown in Philadelphia, Pennsylvania.

Longing for Adulthood

Forrest Gilmore

On my first morning at the edge of Death Valley, I woke to the sound of a banjo playing. Our guide plucked away at the strings. The sun had yet to rise but I could catch a faint glimmer of light on the horizon. There was a bit of tension among the group, myself included, because we knew this was our day. Very soon, each of us would venture out alone to see what four days of solitude and hunger would teach us. I decided to make light of my uneasiness and danced a little step of my own invention to the guide's music, bouncing away to some twangy jig at five o'clock in the morning. Some people laughed and began to dance with me. Some wondered out loud at how I could actually be feeling any joy at the moment.

The sun did eventually show itself. I snapped a photo capturing the light as it pierced the sky and climbed above the mountaintops. It got warm fast, even though we were at seven thousand feet in late September. We packed our gear in a hurry, knowing that we would be leaving soon and that on this day there would be no breakfast. Four days without food seemed like a long time.

With my bag on my shoulder, I walked over to our guide, the banjo man. As I stepped into a circle of stones, he prayed that my journey would go well. He told me, "Pay attention. It will be over before you know it," but I didn't believe him. He spread the smoke of some mountain sage about, hugged me, and sent me on my way. I walked off to four days in the desert, without food, without shelter, without people. I walked off to mark a transition that I felt ready to make and for which I had prepared my whole life. I set out for what is commonly known as a vision quest, an ancient rite of passage used throughout the world to help people make and mark the transition into adulthood.

There is a basic truth that every spiritual traveler knows—death happens more than once in our lives. These small "d" deaths occur when we feel the deep inner pull of our psyches, calling us to let go of who we've been in order to more fully become who we are.

This recurring journey of transformation has a name: positive disintegration. Positive disintegration basically means that every form of life must at some

point shed its current form in order to evolve into a
new and hopefully more adaptable form. Our physical death is the most classic example, the letting go
of our bodies so that other bodies more adaptable to
our world can come into being. But there are many
other positive disintegrations that occur in our lives—
puberty, leaving the family home, the entry into vocation, marriage, parenthood, the death of parents, and
retirement. In the fall of 1998, the season of my vision
quest, I was immersed in one of my own.

Three years earlier and just twenty-four years old, I
moved three thousand miles from my family to begin
my studies for the ministry in California. I entered
seminary ambitious, idealistic, and naïve. I had so little
awareness of what ministry was—even worse, I had
no idea who I was.

Being away from my family and immersed in the
cauldron of seminary allowed me to come into a
greater awareness of myself. I grew up in a home with
an alcoholic, codependent family dynamic that dated
further back than my parents' generation. In order to
cope, I chose to become the family peacemaker, keeping
things calm and safe by being very well behaved and,
at times, quietly nonexistent. I came to see my value by
how I made others feel; if others were at peace, so was
I. If others were not, I was to blame. I was the "good"
boy, defined by external approval. I remember believ-
ing myself to be so much more spiritually advanced

than I was, while at the same time being terrified that someone might discover me to be otherwise.

As I entered seminary, I had no awareness of this. I remember being asked at one point to name some of my personal flaws. So subconsciously fearful of disapproval, I could not name one.

Seminary became a harbor for me, a place of love and encouragement as I explored my depths. I found the space to go within and the care I needed to engage those untended places. While my coursework was of great value, I learned the most between classes, applying my personal learning to the intimate relationships that emerged within my school. I loved and lost. I hurt others and others hurt me. I found the strength to be angry and the courage to ask for forgiveness. I began to shift from the spiritually advanced image I was trying to present to the world to being an actual person—brave, smart, kind, weak, fearful, flawed.

These internal transitions peaked for me during my twenty-seventh year. That spring I completed my academic studies, was accepted into a ministerial internship, the last of my grandparents died, and an important romantic partnership came to an end. In the summer I left the outdoor camp I had worked at since I was sixteen and also was involved in a major car accident. And that fall, as I headed into the desert for a month-long training on wilderness rites of passage, including my four-day solo and fast, I felt my old way of being disintegrate as I deeply longed to become something new.

During this training while preparing for my fast, I learned that my experience was not unique. Cultures throughout the world have traditionally affirmed the sacred journey of death and rebirth that each person must make in order to mature.

Rites-of-passage theory affirms three major transitions between four stages in a person's life—from childhood to adolescence to adulthood to elderhood. While these stages are all profoundly important, the shift to adulthood has been especially emphasized for the health of society. While childhood and adolescence are both appropriately focused on the self, adulthood is a time of offering oneself in service to the larger whole. The adult is the source of life for the culture, the one who provides for people so that they may live. Without the adult, a community falls apart. After years of learning about life, love, frailty, and forgiveness, and on the cusp of entering into the ministry, it was this ancient and essential transition that I sought.

Walking into the desert, I settled into the sacred landscape that was to be my home for the next four days. No grand visions flashed before my eyes while I was there, no holy apparitions spoke words of wisdom to me. I simply sat, allowing myself to slowly settle into the rhythm of the world. Free from the countless distractions of modern life, I watched the passage of the sun through the day and the stars through the night.

In the quietness of the experience, I never felt bored but I did feel a touch of anxiety that grew stronger in certain moments. I recognized the many ways that my life had been like that: a subtle yet persistent frustration with reality. I remember watching the mountains, amazed at their motionless patience with the daily passing of the light.

I thought of countless things—my family, my friends, loved ones, how I've lived my life, how I wanted to live my life in the future, what it meant to be an adult, a man, a minister—and many insights came my way. One in particular struck home: I had lived my life faintly. Seeking to be the peacemaker in my family, I had grown up gentle and kind, but afraid of conflict, of asserting myself, of taking my place. I was highly empathetic and compassionate but rarely brave or strong. In everyday situations, I could be a generous presence, but in the midst of difficulty or conflict I checked out. I tended to be of service to others by diminishing rather than expanding myself.

In my reflections, I read some words that I had brought along with me from deep ecologist John Seed. He writes,

> When humans investigate and see through their layers of anthropocentric self-cherishing, a most profound change in consciousness takes place.

Alienation subsides. The human is no longer an outsider apart. Your humanness is then recognized as merely the most recent stage of your existence, and . . . you start to get in touch with yourself as mammal, as vertebrate, as a species only recently emerged from the rainforest. As the fog of amnesia disperses, there is a transformation in your relationship to other species, and in your commitment to them. . . . *"I am protecting the rainforest" develops to "I am part of the rainforest protecting myself. I am that part of the rainforest recently emerged into thinking."* (italics added)

This quote inspired me. It got me thinking about the power of names. I value and still use the name my parents gave me—Ian. However, for me it recalled my child-self, generous and decent, but meek. I wanted to mark my transition into adulthood in a very tangible way. Taking the name Forrest, in the spirit of "I am part of the rainforest protecting myself, I am that part of the rainforest recently emerged into thinking," honored this shift into adulthood. It reminded me of where I'm from. It affirmed my connection with something so much greater than myself—the forest, the sky, the soil, the water, the animals, the plants, the people, the earth, the stars. It reminded me of the source of my strength—the wondrous existence that brought me into being and nurtured me through my days. Forrest called me forth to use the individuality of my life to bravely and compassionately serve the whole of life. With this change, I honored my past gentleness and kindness, while acknowledging my newly added strength.

On the last night of my fast, I realized it was time to let Ian die so that Forrest could live. Following a simple ritual described to me by our guide, I formed a circle of stones, a metaphorical death lodge that I would remain within until the morning. In some cultures, the death lodge is a place where people go as they prepare to die. Others visit the dying person there one by one, giving each a chance to express his or her sentiments— forgiveness, advice, unfinished concerns, love, farewells. I invited the people I wished to speak with into my imagination and said the things I needed to say in order to feel complete. I voiced many things, but anger was the most significant, as I finally expressed all the bottled-up fury that remained unspoken for so long.

My anxiety grew as I sat there, trapped in that tiny compass of space. Somewhere around midnight, I declared myself dead. For the rest of the night, I kept myself awake, watching the stars cross the sky as I lay in the cocoon of my sleeping bag. I remember how, after making the decision to die, I relaxed completely.

As dark slowly shifted to dawn, I went out to the ledge to watch the sun rise. I sat, staring at the horizon for what seemed like forever. At last, a spark of light appeared, piercing my heart and capturing my breath.

As I felt that first flash of sun, like a gift, I knew with perfect clarity that the word *Forrest*, with all its implied meaning, was to become my new name, and I was to embody that name by constantly remembering where I have come from and to what I belong.

Immersed in the joy of the sun and the declaration of my new name, I realized that my quest had come to an end. I packed my gear and returned to camp. I once again found myself greeted by the smoke of sage and the prayers of the banjo man.

"Thank God, it's over," I said.

"Oh, no," he replied. "It's just begun."

While I can't entirely explain what happened to me in the desert, I am living testimony that the rite worked. The changes in me following the fast were enormous. I found a relationship to something greater than myself, which lives on in me through a blending of kindness and courage that I did not have before.

In the years since, I have had countless opportunities to test the truth of my transition. I have succeeded often, but also failed at times and needed to make amends. I revealed my new name to the world and experienced the judgment of others because "sane" people don't change their names. I confronted my father on his alcoholism and set boundaries that allowed me to stay in relationship with him without enabling his behavior. (As I write this, he's not had a drink for more than eight years.) I found the courage to run into my neighbor's burning apartment, pull him out, help put out the fire, and save the rest of the complex from the blaze. I confessed about and took responsibility for a significant mistake I made in my first ministry. Now, after eight years of ministry, I serve one of our denomination's larger congregations. And at long last, I am preparing to marry the love of my life, while taking on the mantle of "soul daddy" to her two children.

Although these actions and accomplishments serve as markers of the changes I've made, I find the true impact of the fast revealed in my day-to-day interactions—making the hard but healthy decisions, being honest about anger and fear, finding intimacy in imperfection, loving without clinging or distancing, affirming myself while taking responsibility for failure, choosing joy over cynicism.

It seems to me that Western society suffers from a crisis of maturity. Adulthood has come to be viewed not as the life-giving source of our culture but as boring, out-of-touch, and oppressive. Without the inspiration of meaningful adults, our children choose to remain children. And yet for those children wanting more, we have few paths that test and affirm their readiness.

The journey of deepening maturity never truly comes to an end, and I find myself called to give back as I have received, to guide others through their passages as I have been guided. May we all embrace our own longing to take up the mantle of maturity and encourage our children—inspiring, honoring, and supporting them as they take their first steps on the long and wonderful path to adulthood. In this time of great change in our world, when the mature adult is needed more than ever, let us embrace the spirit of sacred adulthood and give of ourselves as a gift to life.

—-—

Forrest Gilmore is parish minister at the Unitarian Universalist Congregation of Princeton, New Jersey.

A Path Diverted

Greg Pelley

In 2001, when my daughter was six months old, my wife and I decided that I would become a stay-at-home dad. I was on a traditional professional career path at the time, having dutifully completed graduate degrees in architecture and construction management. I had completed a three-year internship and I was nearing the end of a grueling battery of examinations needed for an architect's license.

I enjoyed my job and was having fun. I engaged myself in every decision, every process that led to the creation of new environments for people to live, work, and play in. My coworkers and I liked and respected each other. I was married to the woman I loved. We had a house, two cars, and a couple of dogs. I could say without reservation that I had become an adult. A man.

Truthfully, I had shed the child in me long before. The youngest of four kids, I often looked longingly toward growing up. I envied my three sisters for all they apparently knew, for all the choices they got to make. I respected my father for the work he did, tending the sick as a physician in small-town Illinois. I admired my mother for her ability to track everything that was going on in our family, as well as engaging in her own pursuits. It seemed that almost everyone I looked up to was older than I. And that was what I wanted.

When my parents divorced, I was thirteen. I moved with my mother to suburban Phoenix. Well-meaning friends of the family pulled me aside and whispered that I was the "man of the house" now. I internalized those whispers and was excited at the prospect. Finally I had permission, even a demand, to step into the role of an adult. I do not know if that is what those well-meaning whispers meant, or if those friends were only trying to say something, however clichéd, to mask their discomfort with my parents' divorce. Perhaps they were only trying to offer me comfort in those difficult days and weeks. In any case, I heard their words and began to consider all the possibilities that I thought lay in the Adult World—the freedom, the choices, the glory.

I was soon making plans for college and career, not necessarily based on my own dreams, but on some sense of what grown-ups do. Grown-ups make plans, they go to college, get well-paid jobs, marry, and have babies. This was my duty and my destiny. With my parents' divorce, I had been given the green light to shed the vestiges of childhood—wonder, discovery, curiosity, exploration—and get serious about being an adult.

And at thirty years old, I was there. The Man of the House. The loving husband. The professional architect. I could mow the lawn, check the oil, paint the walls, plant the shrubs, cook the supper, wash the clothes, meet with the clients, negotiate with the contractor, and drink the beer. There was no room in my life for my childhood.

Being on such a quick path, the next development was predictable. We had a baby—a beautiful girl we named Sydney. I was a dad. I was enthralled—and unprepared. Having given up on my own childhood so early, I had no context to gauge how a child experiences the world. The typical thoughts ran through my head. Would I be a good father? Do I even know what that means? What if I fail? How can I teach this wondrous creature about the world into which she has been born?

When Sydney was born, my wife and I were both with small firms that valued our contributions enough to work out flexible arrangements so we could keep our daughter out of day care. It seemed that we had created the perfect situation. We were both working professionals and stay-at-home parents.

As wonderful as that all sounded, the reality was far less satisfying. Neither one of us was able to spend

enough time at work to be an integral part of the organizations that employed us. Nor, when we were home,
did we feel fully attuned to the rhythms of raising a
child. We were suffering in both roles, and our greatest
fear was that our child would suffer as well.

After several months, we made a choice. I would
give up my job and be a full-time stay-at-home dad.
While I was determined to make a go of it, I was also
determined not to completely give up my career path. I
was certain I would be able to find the elusive balance
that self-help pop-psychologists promote. To help me
along, within the first few weeks of leaving the architectural firm, I received three separate job offers.

At first, I was annoyed with the offers. It seemed they
just didn't get it. I wasn't leaving the firm because I was
seeking a new job; I was leaving to be a stay-at-home
dad. Secretly, though, the offers boosted my ego. And I
thought that, with so many unsolicited offers, I would
easily be able to slide back into the professional world
once my daughter was older. What I didn't realize is
how pervasive the offers would become, and how they
continually would try to drag me back into that world,
even when I was settled into my new role.

In retrospect, my determination not to give up
completely on my career path is indicative of my lack
of security in the decision to stay at home. Perhaps,
down deep, I even thought I would fail so miserably at
homemaking that Fate, or more likely my wife, would

intervene and send me back into the easy comfort of a career. No matter how progressive I may try to be, or how unconcerned about how my life measures up I appear to be, it turns out I may just be a traditionalist. I am psychologically stuck in the dogma of a "traditional" way of life, even when I intellectually reject that dogma.

Very early in life I had replaced my sense of self-confidence with a concern for others' perceptions of me, of how I dressed, how smart or talented I might be, how I fit in. I never realized how much this was the case until I became a stay-at-home dad and noticed that Sydney wasn't interested at all in what others thought of her. Even today, when something is funny, she laughs. When something is frustrating, she screams. It does not matter where we are or who we may be disturbing.

Through Sydney, I discovered that children don't necessarily care how they are dressed, whether their shirt goes with their pants, or whether their socks match their outfit—or each other. Shoes are an annoyance to be removed at every opportunity. All other considerations are pushed aside; life is to be lived out loud, an experience of unconcerned self-expression.

It would be too easy to just get over myself and bask in the glory of free self-expression. However, so much of my identity has been tied up in my self-consciousness. Those "man of the house" whispers compelled me to invent myself as an adult at thirteen. Lacking actual experience, I just impersonated the adult be-havior around me.

Now, so many years later, my relationships are bound up in an identity based more on observation of others than on personal experience or knowledge. Giv-ing up that self-consciousness for self-confidence means risking all that I have carefully built, though it might stand on shaky ground. It is that risk—that somehow I might become so radically different a man than I have been, that I would lose everything and everyone I care about—that inhibits my living out loud. But, slowly, incrementally, I am trying.

A little more than two years after Sydney was born, our second daughter, Grace, came into this world, and I instantly fell in love again. My full life became even more full, and my new identity began to form—*abu al-banat*, "father of daughters."

One morning last fall, I picked up Grace from pre-school. She was now two and a half years old. When we arrived home, I was rushing to get into the house to do whatever it was I thought had to get done at that moment. When I got to the back door, I turned to see her squatting on the sidewalk, blankie in one hand, poking a stick at something on the ground. Frustrated, I barked at her to get inside *now*. She stood and let the stick drop, still staring at whatever she had been prodding. I impatiently held the door and growled,

"Come *on*, Grace! We *need* to get inside!" She took a half step toward me and cocked her head to one side, her eyes never leaving that spot on the ground.

Suddenly, it hit me. *This* is the clash between being an adult and being a child. At that moment, for Grace, nothing could be more important than what had caught her attention. It was time to wonder, to explore. I sighed, sad that I had given up the ability to be deeply interested in something crawling across the sidewalk on a warm afternoon. I let the door shut, walked the few steps to Grace's side, and quietly asked, "What do you see?" She picked up the stick and pointed. It took a moment for me to quiet down enough for my eyes to see.

An ant was dragging a crumb of bread that looked to be four times its size. The ant pulled and pushed and climbed on top of the crumb, then underneath it. The scene was excruciating, and fascinating. I sat down, and Grace slipped into my lap. She never said a word, keeping the stick in one hand and her blanket clutched in the other, thumb in her mouth. It took several minutes for the ant to move that crumb the last six inches to the edge of the sidewalk, before slipping down into the leaves and out of sight. Grace stood, dropped the stick, and walked up the stairs to the door. I didn't know what to do, what to say. At the top of the stairs, she turned to me and said, "Come *on*, Daddy."

Through my daughters, my sense of exploration has opened up. While I have had a difficult time keeping up with an architectural practice, I have been able to find new things to fascinate and engage me. I have learned to bake bread and to kayak. I have started to appreciate literature more fully. I have developed coursework for college students and leadership-training seminars. I serve the church community. I do these things not for profit or for a resume or for any traditionally adult reasons, but out of a sense of curiosity and wonder, a sense of exploration into new possibilities.

Nonetheless, many people don't see the difference. I have been told that I should open a bakery or a restaurant, that I should write online courses for architects seeking continuing education credits, that I should return to architectural practice, that I should write.

Apparently, it is difficult for some to recognize these endeavors as exploration and wonder for their own sake, instead of potentially profitable opportunities. Perhaps they are only trying to console me in the chaos that comes with parenting, or perhaps they seek to soothe their uneasiness with my identity struggles. In either case, I have learned to listen to my own heart as it finds its childhood rhythm.

Through the lives of my daughters, I have found that I can get back what I gave up when I first heard those long-ago whispers to grow up. I have learned that speaking, thinking, and reasoning as a child are not things to be put away, to be given up for adulthood. These things do not cloud my judgment; they do not fail to be relevant to my sense of self. Instead they add richness to my life and give a sense of newness to every day.

Recently, I took Sydney and Grace to the Des Moines Art Center. I was curious about how they would respond to the art, particularly some of the more abstract pieces. With a sense of exploration, I guided them through and paused only when something caught their eye. Edward Hopper's *Automat* was the first painting they seemed to notice. I quietly sat down on the floor in front of it, and they happily plopped next to me. We sat cross-legged together and looked up at the woman in the painting. They asked me who she was. I asked them where she was and what they thought she was doing. They talked about her yellow hat. I asked if they could figure out what the weather was like outside the dark window behind her. They decided that it was cold and might be raining, and they began to develop her story. Why she seemed sad. Why she was alone. What was in the cup she held. Where she might go when she left the automat. We sat there, the three of us, in wonder, in curiosity, in discovery. We sat there, the three of us, children.

--

Greg Pelley lives in Des Moines, Iowa, and is a member of the First Unitarian Church of Des Moines.

Getting Ready for the Real World

Nathan Ryan

In high school, I was extremely active in Unitarian Universalism. I was president of my church's youth group, a member of the district's Youth Adult Committee, and a liaison to the district's Religious Education Committee. Blessed with a community that encouraged my emotional, spiritual, and leadership development, I knew who I was and what I wanted to be, and I was happy with myself. My friends from Young Religious Unitarian Universalists (YRUU) called this process of self-discovery "coming out of the house." It describes a process that begins whenever your inner strength outweighs the external pressures to conform. For me, that age was seventeen, and I was fortunate to be surrounded by a supportive community that helped to guide and encourage me on my spiritual path. For the first time I had the confidence to live my life proudly as a Unitarian Universalist. This was also the time when I first met Lauren, who would later become my wife.

Lauren and I were lucky enough to meet in an environment quite unlike many other high-school-age cultures. YRUU encouraged deep and intimate platonic relationships with many people while never requiring a sexual commitment. The YRUU community embraced friendships that ignored gender or sexual attraction, helping to lay the groundwork for our marriage to be free from many of the jealousy issues with which other couples struggle. Our shared experience has given us the ability to recognize and foster a healthy relationship.

I first heard my call to ministry while I was part of YRUU. I had never been able to dedicate myself to something I wasn't enthusiastic about, and I found little that lit my passion in the secular world. I knew that I would be happiest working in the church. At the time, though, I thought pulpit ministry was the only option and was concerned that I wasn't inspired by traditional religious experiences such as worship services, meditation, or reading sacred texts.

Church had been central to my life growing up, so it was important that I stay involved at college. However, I had no car, and it was nearly impossible to get to services. A few times I asked someone in the local congregation for a ride, but it made me feel too much like a child. It made me dependent on someone older at a time when I most needed to feel independent. After a while, it became too much of a hassle and an imposition, and I just stopped going.

The energy I had previously spent on church shifted instead to living out the values that Unitarian Universalism had instilled in me. I discovered a thriving community of activists whose social justice activities provided an ideal setting for me to live out those values. Surprised to discover that Baton Rouge was home to such a strong progressive community, I immediately joined many student and community organizations.

I have always considered myself an environmentalist, but I thought that meant caring about the rainforest and other things that were far away and didn't affect people I met in real life. Through my involvement in the Student Environmental Action Coalition (SEAC), I learned that the majority of the chemical plants in Louisiana were located along a seventy-mile stretch of the Mississippi River between Baton Rouge and New Orleans—often near poor and, in many cases, predominantly black neighborhoods. Because of the impact of those chemicals on local health, that area of the state has been called "Cancer Alley." When I saw this environmental racism in action and realized that my state was home to an intentional structure of social injustice, I understood for the first time that some environmentalists are actually fighting to save people's lives.

Working through organizations such as SEAC became my primary preoccupation during college. This emphasis on activism took up so much of my time that very little was left for my faith.

I had assumed that I would go straight to seminary after graduating from college. During my senior year, I flew to Chicago to look at Meadville-Lombard Theological School, one of the Unitarian Universalist divinity schools. I stayed on campus and got to meet a great number of the students. They welcomed me with open arms. I sat in on a few classes and even got to participate in one of their Wednesday night worship services. I had a great time. I was glad for the experience, but my visit left me feeling too young to go to seminary. The students I met were all at least in their late twenties and many were in their forties and fifties. They seemed to be much more at peace in the world than I was. Once back home, I realized that I needed more life experience in order to be an effective minister and decided to take a break from school for at least a few years.

When the next move in your career is as vague as gaining life experience, you have a lot of options. I was lucky enough to be in a situation where it was easy for me to choose one. In college I had attended UU district events and reconnected with Lauren. We dated throughout my last two years of school, and now I was free to move to Austin to be with her.

Once I could afford a car, I tried visiting one of the Unitarian Universalist churches in Austin regularly. For the first few months, I attended the worship service every week. Each time, a different person asked me if I knew what Unitarians were or what they believed. Occasionally someone would turn around and whisper, "Don't worry, the services aren't usually like this." No one I talked with ever assumed that I had heard of Unitarian Universalism, let alone that I had always been UU. I was often treated as though I had just wandered in off the street, as if I hadn't come to the church through my own faith and convictions.

Attending church regularly for the first time in my life validated something I had always known—I don't like worship services. Growing up, I had assumed that I was simply too young to "get it." Now that I was older and had a pretty strong personal theology, I realized that the sit-back-and-listen style of worship didn't speak to me. It certainly didn't feed my soul in the same ways that YRUU or activism did. In fact, the only reason I went to church was that I thought it was the adult thing to do.

To find a place in the church outside the sanctuary, I tried joining committees, without much success. Nobody seemed to want my help except for manual labor. I was given many opportunities to clean dishes or set up tables, but never to share my vision of Unitarian Universalist ministry through worship, facilities, or membership.

Finally, I found a meaningful way to get involved when the director of religious education at the church recruited me as a Sunday-school teacher. Thrilled to find someone dedicated and passionate about the faith, she assigned me to teach the middle-school class. I was equally excited, because she had given me a way to become active in the church and live out my faith. I loved teaching. It got me out of going to the service, while allowing me to help other Unitarian Universalists grow in their faith. I was able to nurture liberal theology and progressive values in children, while working with a group of caring and fun adults. I never expected that sharing my experiences with kids would be so important to my faith development, but it brought out a new excitement and energy that had been missing for me in the larger congregation. I loved helping to grow our faith, and it was a nice break from what I did outside of church.

The best job I had been able to find when I moved to Austin was as a substitute teacher in the public schools, which seemed ideal for my first job after college. I had complete freedom to choose which days I worked and still made enough money to get by. If I had a really terrible day, I could decide never to return to that school. I gained experience working with students of all different ages, backgrounds, and abilities. However, this was only a temporary job, not a career, and nothing about it fed my soul.

Every time I was unable to think on my feet, I was eaten alive by students whose most lofty goal, as far as I could tell, was to make my day as miserable as possible. It was much harder to create a rapport with students in the schools than it was at church. Most of my energy was spent on manipulation rather than honest communication. Teachers who should have been my colleagues generally avoided me, as many established teachers there shunned the subs. I felt unsuccessful and a little embarrassed whenever I told people what I did. My typical explanation at family gatherings seemed to be, "Well, I'm still yelling at kids and not making any positive impact on the world." The only meaningful experiences I had with youth came from my work in the church. After two years, I decided I'd had enough. I quit substituting even though I had no prospect of a better job, and I spent an entire summer unemployed.

During the time I was subbing, I taught Sunday school with a woman who served as the religious education administrator. She was leaving the church that fall and asked if I would consider applying for her job. I was flattered—this kind of opportunity could not have come at a better time. I spent eight months working alongside the director of religious education. She did most of the planning, and I did most of the nuts-and-bolts work, but every day I woke up excited to do my job and be a part of the mission of the church.

Throughout my time as administrator, the director subtly began assigning to me more and more of her own job duties. She asked me to determine future projections of classroom needs, begin planning the summer program, and evaluate teaching teams. Although I was not aware of it at the time, she was training me as her replacement. A few months later she resigned and I was promoted.

Finally able to pursue a career in Unitarian Universalism, I entered this job full of enthusiasm. I found myself in an ideal position to give the kids in my church the tools to understand and succeed in the outside world. I taught them the importance of our church's history and heritage, and I found many different ways to inspire our congregation to live out its ministry. I was in an awkward position, however, because, on quite a few occasions, church members openly questioned my ability to do my job, assuming that at the age of twenty-four, I couldn't possibly have adequate experience. It was a challenge to make difficult professional decisions—recommending disciplinary action to parents or asking a teacher to step down because of an unhealthy interaction—when many congregants knew that I was no older than their own children. I found myself dressing and acting beyond my years in order to garner the respect that most of my colleagues received automatically.

My gender was also an issue. When I was hired, I was the only male to hold this type of position in the state of Texas. At every training or conference, I was surrounded by women, causing me to wonder whether our faith has made the same egalitarian strides in religious education ministry as it has in pulpit ministry. I also felt I was given more respect than many of my female colleagues. My congregation deferred to my desire not to perform tasks that had little to do with religious education, such as playground duty and babysitting. I knew that some other religious educators were not given the same privilege, and many of my colleagues felt that their congregations were less respectful of them as professionals than their ministerial counterparts. My experiences gave me much insight into the hidden gender inequities between what is typically considered a man's job (preaching) and what is still viewed as women's work (education).

Were it not for my early experiences in Sunday school, I would not have the foundation for the liberal theology and socially progressive views I hold today. Were it not for YRUU, I would not have the convictions to live out my values and be proud of my faith, and I certainly would not have met my wife. Were it not for colleagues who inspired me, I would not have had the confidence to teach religious education or become a director myself. I attribute most of who I am and where I am today to my involvement in the Unitarian Universalist church and, more specifically, its religious education ministry.

Several years ago a friend related the Japanese legend that says that after you fold a thousand paper cranes, your wish for peace and serenity will be granted. Although I doubted this claim, it seemed like a neat thing to try. As it turned out, I really enjoyed origami because it gave me something to do with my hands, and afterward, I always had a small gift in my pocket for someone who needed cheering up.

After three years, I eventually finished folding a thousand cranes. Logically, I know that folding little pieces of paper should not determine my happiness, but my heart has never understood logic. All it knows is this: When I started folding paper cranes, I was a miserable substitute teacher, far away from my professional and religious identity. When I finished the last crane, at General Assembly 2005, I was a happy director of religious education at a wonderful church, living out my personal calling and ministry. Along the way, I became more satisfied, more at peace, and more serene. I have always found happiness in the little things, and I believe that regardless of the source from which we draw meaning, what matters is that every generation in our faith can receive the same gifts that mine has.

——

Nathan Ryan is the religious education administrator at the First Unitarian Church of Dallas, Texas.

The Ties That Bind

Scott Gerard Prinster

Tying my necktie almost always leads to thoughts of my father. Now that I wear a tie a few times a week for work, he's on my mind regularly. Neckties have become a reminder of how persistent the connection is between the two of us, and of the forces that guide boys to become men.

It was not my father who taught me how to tie a necktie, but the resident assistant across the hall from me in our dormitory at Purdue University. I was working in the dorm dining room and had become a manager-in-training, which meant that I would be wearing a necktie under the maroon manager's jacket when I supervised the student crew. On the few occasions when I wore a tie in high school, my father had tied it for me, and once at a speech contest I even had to ask a female classmate to help me. Somehow, I arrived at college without knowing how to tie one myself.

The training for dining-room managers, which bore some resemblance to fraternity hazing, began with the realization that I couldn't figure out this basic test of manhood on my own. As with so many other pieces of manly knowledge, I was convinced that other sophomores had already completed this rite of passage and were flaunting their own neckties just to remind me how far behind I was. Our RA, however, was a genuinely nice guy and didn't seem at all surprised that I hadn't yet mastered the skill. When I knocked on Joe's door with tie draped across my shoulders, he and a friend broke off their conversation to walk me through the process. "The secret," he said, "is to start by tying a triangle; the smaller and tighter it is, the neater the knot will be." I practiced the triangle and the final knot with him a few times, and then a few more times in the privacy of my own room. In the twenty years since that lesson, tying a necktie has been a regular activity that now requires no real effort.

It's probably already clear that a necktie was more to me than a simple piece of clothing. In my sophomore year I also came out as a gay man, and the fall semester was a completely hellish prologue to the act of coming out itself. I alternated between immersing myself in my studies and withdrawing into self-loathing. My life careened through those months before lurching off its neatly planned path entirely. I couldn't bring myself to speak to my parents about this truth that I could no longer ignore, suppress, or destroy. They only knew that I was exhausted and unhappy on the occasions I visited home. Learning how to tie a necktie from my RA was just further evidence that I shouldn't turn to my father for help. Being in college meant that I was on my own, and that I should have known by then what it means to be a man. My father was a redneck, Republican, deer-hunting, beer-drinking, country-music-listening bear of a man, and my being gay was just one more thing that separated us. Other men in my life, like Joe across the hall and friends in the gay community, would have to serve as guides and teachers in his place.

My studies sometimes distracted me from the process of coming out, and from the unhappiness that I couldn't force myself to be someone other than who I was. As a physics major, I studied the basic principles that drive the world—mass, distance, force, velocity. I learned that electricity and magnetism are just two expressions of one phenomenon, the same one that also produces light. I learned that gravity is a force that attracts all bodies toward one another and grows weaker with increasing distance, but is never reduced to nothing. As my brain tried to make sense of the physical world, my heart likewise struggled with the lessons of the inner life.

In *The Myth of Maturity*, Terri Apter explores the isolation and frustration that many young adults face, especially as they navigate the threshold of college life. Partly because the rites of passage into adulthood are becoming less clear-cut, Apter believes, young adults are increasingly puzzled and overwhelmed at what they think is expected of them. While fifty years ago adulthood generally meant completing relatively straightforward rites of passage—graduation, employment, marriage, children—today these tasks may be stretched out over as many as twenty years.

Convinced that adulthood means *knowing* the rules and painfully aware of their perceived shortcomings, young adults suffer silently or in outbursts of frustration and anger. Their clueless and unhelpful parents remember their own young adulthood and its relatively unambiguous thresholds all crossed before age twenty-five, and assume that it is best for their young adult sons and daughters to work it out themselves.

By the time my father was the age I am now, his son was nearly off to college. I can scarcely imagine raising a teenager of my own, and yet my father managed to do it, despite my characterization of him as a redneck conservative beer-drinker. Recently, I served as the UU minister at the University of Wisconsin campus. Among the students I worked with were young men navigating that daunting journey into adulthood. I was privileged to serve as a mentor for many of them, and I now have much more compassion for my father and the difficulty of his task.

When I went off to college three hundred miles away from home, I assumed that I was leaving behind the pull of small-town life, my blue-collar family, and all of the qualities in my father I had identified as faults. However, for people, the gravity between two distant bodies is not diminished by the miles between them; the force returns as strong as before. Now that I cross into middle adulthood, I am surprised to realize the similarities between my father and me. I've inherited his temper—and his back hair, of all things. All the buttons but one on my car radio are set to country music stations, and I play fiddle and go two-stepping every Monday evening. I drink more beer than I probably should, and one day I did a double take in front of the mirror, noticing how much I now look like him. I haven't become a Republican, and in fact am too liberal even for many Democrats, but this is also because of my father's influence—while he used to have to shoplift so that we would have meat on the table, I have spent my adulthood rarely wanting for anything, and could develop a political identity based on security and comfort. Again and again, I have to acknowledge how deeply I am rooted in my father's presence and influence.

I've also come to see that manhood is a changing state rather than a fixed set of qualities. In older adulthood, the man my father has become is almost nothing like the caricature I once created. Last week he left a phone message telling me that he was drinking green tea from the coffee company I had introduced him to. *Green tea?* Maturity has made us increasingly alike, and I'm grateful that my father is now both a man I like and one I don't mind being like.

Religious liberals often rankle at the idea that our destiny is set by a power greater than ourselves, that we might not completely control the direction of our lives. But there is much about us that we cannot reason away or change by force of will. The puzzle of our identities is more complex than we want to admit.

My mind comes full circle to this truth as I tie my necktie for our Saturday afternoon worship service. If I give too much attention to the task, my fingers hesitate and fumble until I withdraw my focus and let them do it from memory. A tight and tidy triangle, then a finished knot, and I am ready to greet the congregation, among them the young men hungering for confidence and clarity as I once did. A tight and tidy triangle, composed of my father and me, in relationship with the other men who stood by me as mentors and companions. An enduring knot that binds us to our origins and to the men who have made us who we are.

——

Scott Gerard Prinster is a Unitarian Universalist minister and a doctoral student at the University of Wisconsin–Madison, focusing on the relationship between religion and science.

The Call of Self

Manish K. Mishra

Everything is done in a rush in American culture today. We frantically eat a few bites of lunch before running to our next meeting. We shop at megastores where anything and everything is quickly available. Our news is delivered to us in thirty-second snapshots; anything longer might not retain our attention. We are constantly in a hurry to get somewhere or get something done.

As a young adult in the 1990s, I too was in a rush—a rush to grow up. I wanted my "life" to begin, and I wanted all the pieces in place that would allow that to happen—a career, a life partner, a house, and (if I could manage it) even pets and kids. I wanted solidity and stability. I wanted my life to look and feel like an adult life.

Around me, I saw my twenty-something peers falling into two broad camps. There were those who wanted the roles and responsibilities of adulthood as soon as humanly possible, and others who wanted to try out different roles and see how they fit.

From my younger perspective, this latter group was composed of commitment-phobes. "Ah," I would think, "if only they could get their acts together, they could get an early start in building their 401Ks and working their way up corporate ladders."

Unlike them, I wanted my life to have all the pieces in place. I wanted stability and lunged after it with enthusiasm, even abandon. I was what might colorfully be called a "dumb ass," naïve and inexperienced, and too clueless to recognize it. Outwardly an adult, I lacked much internally. Perhaps most important, I was basing major life decisions on emotions rather than logic.

Most decisions involve some combination of rationality and emotionality, and drawing on emotions is not necessarily a problem. But it helps to explore the quality and the nature of these emotions, which can sometimes cause us to rush ahead for the wrong reasons. Reevaluating our motivations can provide a lens through which to view the twenty-something experience. Young adulthood is such a fragile testing ground—what did we not quite understand in our twenties and why? In my case, the issues of vocation and intimacy drove me to reexamine my life, the world around me, and how I understood both.

In 1993, just a few weeks after graduating from Georgetown University, I began what I expected to be a lifelong career as a diplomat. At virtually the same time, I entered what I believed would be my one committed relationship. At the tender age of twenty-two, I thought I had solved the major life quests—work and human connection.

I was professionally successful throughout my twenties. In the span of just eight years, I was honored twice by the U.S. State Department for my accomplishments; I helped set foreign policy goals and priorities; I traveled the world promoting human rights and the interests of my country; I hobnobbed with foreign dignitaries and was given VIP treatment wherever I went. I was a "tenured" diplomat, on the fast track.

When I decided to leave, the most common reaction was disbelief. Others couldn't understand why I would possibly want to go, but I was unhappy, unexpectedly and deeply so.

My initial exposure to diplomacy was through an uncle who had served as the Indian Ambassador to the United Nations in the 1970s. I remember, as an elementary-school-aged kid, visiting my uncle and aunt in New York City and being whisked away from the airport by a black limousine that took us to a penthouse suite on Park Avenue. I had watched *The Jeffersons*, so I knew that having a "deluxe apartment in the sky" was a big deal. I turned to my mom and asked her what my uncle did. She said he was an ambassador. I had never heard the word before, and she explained that "an ambassador is someone who makes peace in the world."

I was sold, hook, line, and sinker. This sounded like a noble profession, one in which I could utilize my cross-cultural experience—and I'd get to live like Lady Di! This *had* to be the career for me.

I knew my parents hoped that their eldest son would go into one of the prestigious, "preapproved" Indian professions—doctor, corporate executive, engineer, computer scientist, or lawyer. The only problem was that I didn't have the faintest interest in any of those vocations.

A diplomatic career gave me hope that I could do meaningful work and still meet my culture's expectations. But I continued to fear, on some level, the possibility of total rejection. There was still a part of me that longed for cultural approval of my career choice, and I hoped it would come once I had established myself.

Motivated partly by the desire to conform, partly by the fear of rejection, there was also part of me that wanted to live overseas in exotic, faraway locations because then I could get as far away from my immediate family as possible. My parents' relationship was the troubled product of a Hindu arranged marriage, a tradition in which harmonious star charts are more important than personal compatibility. I hoped that if

I were physically distant, I'd be less enmeshed in the family drama. Joining the diplomatic corps was my own version of running away to join the circus.

What I had not tapped into, however, was *who I am*, and how that might inform my experience of vocation. I had matched my career with externally driven needs. Those needs began to feel very different from those of my soul, which I had never really thought about.

In reality I hated living overseas and I hated frequent moves, yet I had signed up for a career in which I could live in dozens of countries over the course of a lifetime. I was at my core a homebody, in the worst possible vocation for a homebody. An openly gay man, I was dedicating my life's labor to an employer (the U.S. government) that has treated, and continues to treat, gay and lesbian employees and their families as second-class citizens. I had also been drawn to diplomacy because it seemed that my uncle was making a difference in the lives of others. Years into doing this work, I found such moments to be relatively rare. I was primarily a glorified paper-pusher, not an agent of cross-cultural understanding and peace. My chosen vocation, in so many fundamental ways, was not "me."

In addition, I was on my way to a better, more meaningful relationship with my parents, and no longer felt the need to run away from home. I also began to realize that I was willing to trade in prestige to be happier. By the late 1990s, I began to realize that I had spent my high school career, my undergraduate years, and now a significant chunk of my adulthood in pursuit of a career that was a bad fit for me. As I absorbed this, I was also left wondering "Where do I go from here?"

At the time, I attended All Souls Church in Washington, D.C., where Rev. Terry Sweetser was the interim senior minister. I found myself in the pews, Sunday after Sunday, appreciating what an incredibly positive influence Terry was, and I began reflecting on whether this might be the type of role I had always hoped to play—embodying, as a minister, our communal hopes for love, care, and understanding.

I gradually moved toward a career in ministry, which felt deeply counter-cultural to me. At the time, I knew of no Unitarian Universalist ministers of Hindu origin. In addition, I struggled with the idea that ministry is not a real profession. Of course it is real and there are other UU-Hindu ministers, but I fought with the internalized voices of my culture objecting to a nontraditional career, one that was unlikely to hold the keys to wealth, prestige, or privilege.

By this point in time, however, I was so unhappy in my diplomatic career that continuing to listen to the logic of my younger self and my internalized cultural values was no longer feasible. My soul was yearning for a vocation in which my fullest self could gain expression. I found that path, and it led me towards ministry.

Even as we long to nurture our individuality, we also long for community and for rich, meaningful partnerships or marriages. I set about this task with as much verve and conviction as I had brought to my pursuit of vocation.

I had come out of the closet at twenty and by twenty-two had decided that experience in romantic relationships was not important for making a decision about a life partnership. Having had only two significant dating experiences as an openly gay man, I settled down with a life partner.

Coming out of a culture with a history of arranged marriages, I had come to believe, mostly subconsciously, that any two people could make a go of it in a partnership or marriage if they were deeply committed to one another. And why not? Over history, millions, if not billions, of Indians had married total strangers and made meaningful lives together. While I did not necessarily believe that complete strangers could make a marriage work, it did seem that a marriage or partnership could succeed if the two people knew one another, deeply cared for one another, and were mutually committed to the goal of life partnership. If that was true, which I believed it was, why date countless individuals? Why not find one person you really care about and love, and make a mutual, life-long commitment to one another? In the profound wisdom of my young adulthood I had thus re-worked

Hindu assumptions about arranged marriage into a palatable, slightly more flexible, gay-friendly format, one that made sense to me at the time.

It was the summer of 1993, and I was soon to be sent overseas on my first diplomatic assignment. Excited at the prospect, I was also intimidated by the thought of leaving Washington, the city where I had discovered that romantic relationships were possible for me. I did not want to lose the sense of connection and community I had found there. I was afraid of feeling alone again.

I wanted to share my new career with someone special, a partner. I pinned my hopes for companionship, partnership, and marriage on my best friend at the time, also a gay professional. It made perfect sense to take this relationship deeper and at my urging we did.

Our friends held us up as an example of true partnership in male-male relationships. We were professionally successful, attractive, supportive of each other's careers, socially comfortable in each other's circles, and deeply caring and loving. We communicated well, we matched one another intellectually, and we had fun together.

There was only one problem. I was completely incapable of fidelity. I began cheating on my partner almost immediately and continued to do so for many years. I felt deep shame, especially because I recognized that my behavior mimicked the patterns of conflict between my father and mother. Even as a young kid, I had vowed never to treat another human being that way—with lies and deceit—and here I was doing exactly that. On top of that shame was heaped confusion as to why a seemingly perfect relationship wasn't perfect.

I wondered if I could ever be monogamous. At the same time, I knew that I didn't want an open relationship, even though I was giving myself such privileges.

The confusion, guilt, and shame became overwhelming. At the age of twenty-six I started psychotherapy, which continued for many years and became the basis for my ongoing practice of self-reflection. I've come to appreciate that understanding ourselves well requires a lifelong commitment.

What eventually became clear to me was that my partner and I processed emotions very differently. I was primarily emotional, and he was intellectual. At times, I literally could not understand how his mind worked, and I'm sure the same was true the other way around. I did not want physical intimacy in a relationship where I felt somewhat alien and misunderstood. And so I sought it elsewhere, in casual relationships, where less was at stake.

After eleven years together, and a legal marriage in the state of Massachusetts, I finally saw that I had repeated the same patterns in my personal life that I had followed in my work life. I entered into a life partnership on the basis of cultural assumptions to which I had given disproportionate weight. I had been significantly motivated by fear and had not taken the time to discover my true self.

Since my separation and divorce, I've had to pick up some of the tasks I left behind in my early twenties—learning how to date, learning what I need from others, learning who I am alone as well as in a relationship. To my surprise, one of my early discoveries has been that I am capable of being monogamous. Though I had never experienced pure monogamy in my marriage, in my subsequent relationships I've discovered that, for me, the ability to emotionally connect with another is the glue that makes monogamy not only possible but meaningful. This understanding, so elusive in my twenties, now makes perfect sense.

In my rush to grow up, I lost sight of what actually motivated me. Sifting through the pieces of the puzzle rationally was not difficult, but it was insufficient. The harder part was figuring out the emotions at play. Was I motivated by fear of failure? By loneliness? By unresolved conflict from my childhood? By a desire to be recognized as an adult?

These are complex questions, and the support of other people can provide a powerful witness for us as we seek the answers. In my case, therapists and ministers helped me, but many can offer the love, care, and expertise needed. It is important to remember that we are never alone unless we allow ourselves to be.

In my thirties I've come to appreciate that there isn't just one way to grow up. Some people were early committers as I was; others dabbled and experimented. But no matter which route we took, many of us made choices in our twenties that didn't work out. We learned from our struggles and mistakes, and we are now more in touch with ourselves as a result.

I know this has been true for me, and because of it, I wouldn't change a thing about how my life has unfolded. My life has been made richer because of my struggles and my mistakes—and the ways I've learned about myself through dealing with them. When it comes to growing up, we will all get there eventually, even if it takes a lifetime.

—-—

Manish K. Mishra is minister of the Unitarian Universalist Church of Saint Petersburg, Florida.

Discussion Questions

1.   Forrest Gilmore writes about his time in the desert as a "positive disintegration" that marked a transition from one phase of life into another. What rites of passage have you experienced? How did these rites help you move into maturity?

2.   The themes of loneliness and solitude appear often throughout the book. What is the difference between the two? What different roles have loneliness and solitude played in your own experience of growing up?

3.   Based on your reading of the essays, what are the particular challenges and blessings that Unitarian Universalism contains for young men? For you? How might this differ from more traditional communities of faith?

4.   Anthony David quotes the Biblical story of Jacob and the angel—"I will not let you go until you bless me." How does that statement apply to your own experience?

5.   How has your father, and/or the experience of becoming a father, influenced the choices you have made?

6.   How does the quest for vocation both help and hinder young men as they grow toward maturity? What has your experience been?

7.   How does disillusionment, even if very painful, help these men begin to realize what matters most to them? Has this ever happened to you?

8.   Do you believe this book would have, or could have, been written forty or fifty years ago? Why or why not?

9.   Several of these essays contain the idea that maturity means growing up and growing younger simultaneously. What do you think the writers mean? What has your experience been?

10.   How does the experience of home shape the writers' reflections? What homes are lost, and what homes are found in their writing? What has home meant to you throughout your life?